S0-FKH-035

Learning Horseback Riding

This book was given to me by: ....

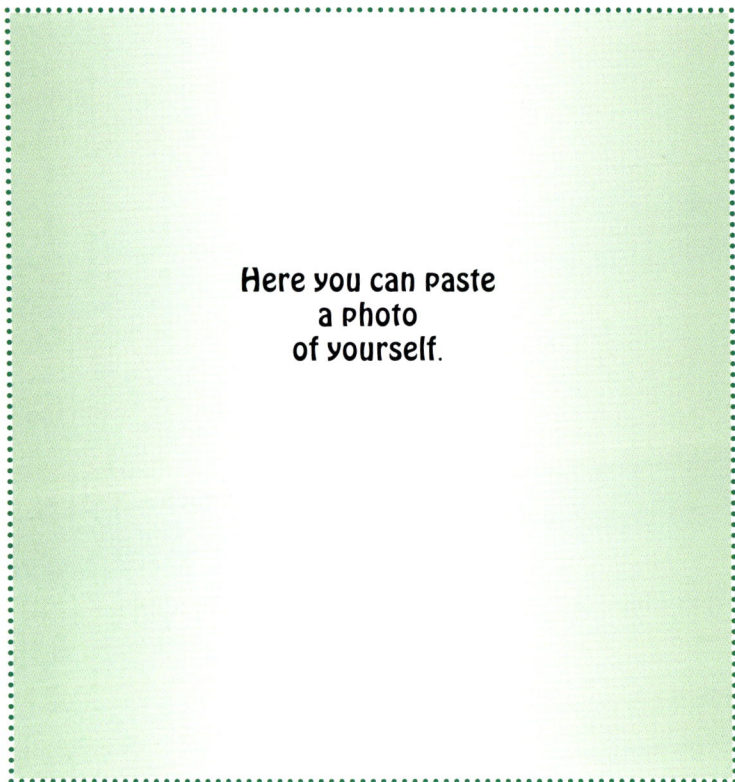

**Here you can paste
a photo
of yourself.**

My name: ....

My birthday: ....

My address: ....

....

Learning
Horseback Riding

Barth/Sieber

Sports Science Consultant:
Dr. Berndt Barth

**MEYER
& MEYER
SPORT**

The authors would like to thank
the Education Department of the German Equestrian Association,
"Reiterliche Vereinigung" (FN) in Warendorf, Germany, and Michael Putz,
distinguished trainer, educator, long time director of riding and driving
schools, as well as author of numerous professional articles, for his expert
advice and support.

Original Title: *Ich lerne Reiten*
Aachen: Meyer & Meyer 2003
Translated by Susanne Evens, Petra Haynes
AAA Translation, St. Louis, Missouri, USA
www.AAATranslation.com

British Library Cataloguing in Publication Data
A catalogue record for this book is available from the British Library

Learning Horseback Riding
Katrin Barth / Antonia Sieber
Oxford: Meyer & Meyer Sport (UK) Ltd., 2005
ISBN 1-84126-153-X

All rights reserved, especially the right to copy and distribute,
including the translation rights. No part of this work may be reproduced –
including by photocopy, microfilm or any other means –
processed, stored electronically, copied or distributed in any form whatsoever
without the written permission of the publisher.

© 2005 by Meyer & Meyer Sport (UK) Ltd.
Aachen, Adelaide, Auckland, Budapest, Graz, Johannesburg,
New York, Olten (CH), Oxford, Singapore, Toronto
Member of the World
Sports Publishers' Association (WSPA)
www.w-s-p-a.org
Printed and bound by: TZ Verlag, Germany
ISBN 1-84126-153-X
E-Mail: verlag@m-m-sports.com

TABLE OF CONTENTS

Caution:
The exercises and practical suggestions in this book have been carefully chosen and reviewed by the authors. However, the authors are not liable for accidents or damage of any kind incurred in connection with the contents of this book.

Hi there, horse lover and beginning rider!
I am Max, and I am an expert on horses.
No wonder, since I belong
to the same big horse family.

I will guide you through this book, and I will be
present in all of the chapters.
I will accompany you during your first encounters with horses
and will assist you with your first riding attempts.

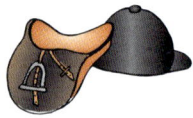

You will see these pictures of me quite often:

When you see this picture, it means that I have a suggestion or a tip for you.

Pretty tricky! The question mark means you can answer the questions or solve puzzlers. The solutions and answers are at the end of the book on the answers page.

Next to this picture are exercises you can do at home. There are many ways to get prepared for riding lessons.

Here is something to record or fill in. Use a pencil if you're not real sure or if you want to keep your entries current.

· · · · · · · · · · · · · · ·1 DEAR BEGINNING HORSEBACK RIDER

Are you one of those people who always stops and longingly watches the horses in every horse pasture? Are you captivated by these big, beautiful, and friendly animals? Then the "horse bug" must have bitten you, too! Maybe your friends are already in a riding club and they have always raved about the horses and riding. Or you watched successful dressage riders and show jumpers on television. Or are you possibly one of the lucky ones who has his own horse at home?

It doesn't matter how the "horse bug" got hold of you.
You have definitely chosen a wonderful sport.

The special thing about riding is that your partner, the horse, is always there with you. You can't forget it during most of the things you do. Good nutrition matters to the rider and the horse. Both require the right equipment, warming up before lessons, and lots of patience and time when learning new things.

You will soon realize how much horseback riding has to offer. You will learn about the special bond between man and horse, adjusting to each other, and affection. You will need patience and endurance, and sometimes willpower, when learning new techniques. It is fun to practice with other children and compete against each other at events.

Maybe someday you will be a successful rider in your favorite discipline. But being well trained as a rider and knowledgeable about horses and their care is important, even if you don't want to become a World Champion or Olympic Champion.

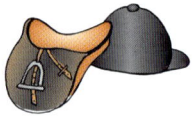

Here are some reasons why kids like to go horseback riding.

What applies to you? Mark "Yes" or "No"!

	Yes	No
I love horses.	☐	☐
I like being at the barn.	☐	☐
I want to take care of horses.	☐	☐
I want to be able to ride.	☐	☐
I like playing with other children.	☐	☐
I have fun working with horses.	☐	☐
I want to jump over obstacles.	☐	☐
I want to be able to do dressage.	☐	☐
I want to go on trail rides.	☐	☐
I want to be better than the others.	☐	☐
My friends can ride, too.	☐	☐
I want to become a professional horseback rider.	☐	☐

If you answered most of these questions with "Yes" you have chosen the right sport.

You need to spend much time with horses and practice a lot. Every rider knows that even on "just" a trail ride being able to stay on the horse's back isn't enough.

Because horseback riding is so popular, there are many books about horses, their care, and techniques. As a horse fan, you surely already have some of these. This particular book is meant to be your companion during those first years of horseback riding. We want to help you in your interaction with horses and with learning the various techniques. Here, you can review things you have learned, as well as get suggestions for practicing at home, and obtain tips for practice sessions and competitions. If this book belongs to you, fill out, check off, and add photos. Have fun with the puzzles.

If something in the book is different from the way your riding instructor has explained it to you, just ask him or her about it. Sometimes there are different schools of thought.

So have a great time with learning to ride and with this book!

– The authors and Max

*Here, you can paste a photo
of your favorite horse.*

. . . . .2 FROM THE LONG HISTORY OF MAN AND HORSE

How the horse became our partner

Nowadays, horses are man's partners. But it wasn't always that way. A long time ago, people even hunted horses to eat them. They needed to do this to survive. Soon, people discovered that horses can be ridden and that this would make them faster hunters. For the first time, the horse became man's partner. Soon, people relied on the horse's strength for pulling carriages and plows.

But then cars were invented and the tractor began pulling the plow across the field. So the horse continued to become less important to man's survival. But people didn't just forget about the horse and push it aside. No, because horses are so loyal and also good looking, they quickly became man's recreational partner. Actual sports using the horse were developed: dressage, show jumping, and much more.

Did you know ...

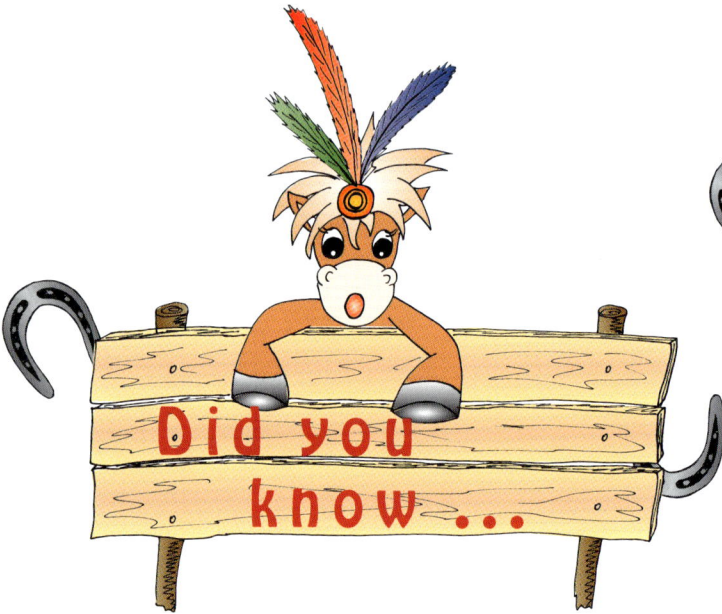

... that 60 million years ago, the ancient horse was approximately one foot tall and had a striped camouflage coat? It is called "Eohippus" and looked more like a cat or a fox.

... that the horse has been serving man for more than 5,000 years?

... that the horse's great-great-great-grandfather came from North America?

... that the black stripe some ponies have on their backs is called "dorsal stripe"? It stems from the ancient wild horses.

... that in the past, monarchs considered the horse a symbol of might and power? They often had themselves painted with horses, had bronze statues made, or upon their deaths had their horse buried with them.

... that there are few free roaming wild horse herds left in the world? Among them are, for instance, the American mustangs.

... that during the Middle Ages, the horse had to be particularly stout? Otherwise it would not have been able to carry the knight with all of his heavy iron armor.

... that dressage was on the Olympic program for the first time at the 1912 Olympics in Stockholm, Sweden? The three basic gaits had to be shown in a ten-minute program. This was followed by five jumps.

... that Germany's male and female dressage riders have almost always been team Olympic Champions since 1936?

... that a horse's height is not measured from the ground up to its ears, but rather to its "withers" (that's the highest point of the back behind the mane).

... that

Write down anything really interesting or amazing you know in the empty box.

Do you remember how many horseshoes were pictured on the previous two pages? Don't go back to look just yet, but try to guess the number!
Write it down here.

Equine associations

In many countries, horseback riders, trainers, and horse breeders have the option to join an equine association in their region or country. These associations offer them lots of support in their work.

- An equine association exists to preserve, promote, and perpetuate any particular breed of horse.
- Equine associations keep track of horse registers; they provide information on scientific and technological advances in the equine industry, and offer publications on the various horse breeds.
- Equine associations sponsor horse shows, training seminars, and other horse-related events.

Which equine association do you know of?

Write it down here:

Here, you can paste or draw the association logo.

If you want to know more, check out the Internet:

http://www.usef.org

or:

Riding at a club

The best way to learn horseback riding is at a club or a riding school. You'll most certainly enjoy spending your free time there, and you'll quickly make friends among the other riders.

To make sure your first riding attempt will be a pleasant experience and that you will enjoy horseback riding for a long time to come, choosing the right club is very important. If there are different riding clubs in your area, visit them with your parents. They should have well-trained lesson horses for beginners that are friendly and trustworthy and will perform all exercises attentively and patiently. Look at the barn aisles and the stalls. Ask to see the area where beginners can practice. What are the riding instructors like? Are there children in your age group?

Ask friends and acquaintances about their experiences and for their recommendations.

Think about what you want and what you need to pay attention to. Take a look at different riding stables and mark an "x" on your list if you are satisfied. Then you'll be able to make an unhurried decision at home.

	1st stable	2nd stable	3rd stable
The horses are handled gently.	☐	☐	☐
The horses look well cared for and seem content.	☐	☐	☐
The horses approach people in a trusting manner.	☐	☐	☐
The stalls and barn aisles look pleasant and clean.	☐	☐	☐
The stalls are large enough and have plenty of light and shavings in them.	☐	☐	☐
The tack looks neat.	☐	☐	☐
The riding instructor is friendly and patient.	☐	☐	☐
There are plenty of children in my age group.	☐	☐	☐
Aside from riding lessons there are other offerings (camp, theoretical instruction, …).	☐	☐	☐
	☐	☐	☐
	☐	☐	☐

My club

If you have already joined a club, write it down here:

Name of your riding stable/club:

Here, you can draw or paste your riding stable's or club's logo:

Name of riding instructor:

Cross out the items you should not feed to a horse!

Oats

Pellets

Which horse belongs in which stall?

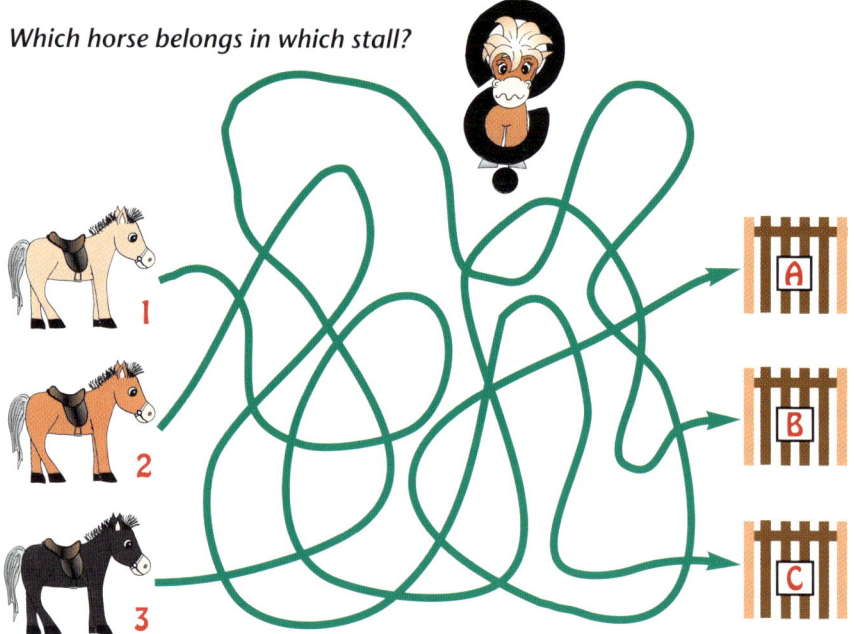

1

2

3

A

B

C

·········3 HELLO, ISABELL WERTH!

Dressage rider and repeated European, World, and Olympic Dressage Champion

Born: July 23, 1969
Home: Rheinberg/Niederrhein, Germany
Occupation: Attorney

How did you get involved with horseback riding?

I grew up with horses on my parents' farm. I started taking lessons on my horse "Funny" at a riding club when I was very young, and over the years, I have been riding more and more. Some time later, I was discovered as a new talent and had the great fortune of being sponsored and trained.

What do you think is so great about horseback riding?

The thing that is so fascinating and special about our sport is the teamwork with the horses. I love horses. It is always so impressive to see horse and rider become one entity and perform the most difficult lessons with the utmost ease and perfection.

I like the competitiveness at competitions. But I also like just being around a horse, taking a trail ride and leaving all worries behind.

You are a very successful rider. What's your secret?

There is no secret. To be successful, you have to love horses, work with them, and train diligently. Of course, you must also have aptitude and talent for horseback riding. But you can't make it on your own. I had an excellent teacher, a superb trainer, and I had access to fabulous horses. In addition, I have a super team taking care of my horses.

Has it always been fun for you?

Yes, and it is still fun. Horses define my life, and every day, I look forward to being with them. There are of course days when I don't feel like working. Then we just hang out, go on trail rides, or use the lunge line. But, as a rider, you are responsible for your horse. You have to make sure it is fed regularly, groomed, and exercised. Moreover, I was determined to become a good rider. For that, I have to practice regularly and in a disciplined manner.

You have been repeated European, World, and Olympic Champion. Why do you go on?

The titles aren't the only reason you do a sport. It's not just about collecting medals and trophies. I just think it is fun. Training young

horses, the competitiveness of tournaments, and the horse shows are fun and challenging. I continue to have new goals and want to move ahead with young horses.

Do you have any other hobbies?

Riding is, of course, my favorite hobby and takes up a lot of my time. But there are other things in my life. I like to read, listen to music, and get together with my friends. It helps me to relax and get away from it all. Getting a good degree and learning an interesting profession was also always important to me.

Do you have a tip for our young riders?

Spend a lot of time around horses, get to know them and take care of them. It is important to build a natural relationship with a horse and learn the proper handling. Next, you should ride as much as possible with regular instruction. To be successful, you need talent, love of the sport, a little luck, and a lot people to support you.

Thank you for this conversation and lots of luck in the future!

Use this space for autographs from successful equestrians.
You can also add photos.

. . . . .4 No Pain, No Gain

Surely you have dreamt of being the best. You ride elegantly, confidently, and error free. No one can guide your horse better than you. Everyone gazes at you in admiration as you ride by.

Or are you imagining yourself with a trophy in your hand and the winner's ribbon on your horse, accepting congratulations from your friends, your riding instructor, and your parents?

But stop! Lying in the grass daydreaming isn't good enough! If you want to be a good rider, maybe even be better than the others, you have to practice often and diligently. That's not always easy, and it may not be real fun right away.

Diligence comes before success!

Goals

When you start learning to ride, you should answer the following questions:

1 What is my goal?

2 With what can I reach my goal?

3 How can I reach my goal?

1 **What is my goal? What am I trying to achieve?**

Taking care of a horse, gaining its trust and riding it is a wonderful feeling. Maybe it would be enough for you to know how to get up on a horse, how to stay on for an extended period of time and then get off voluntarily and gently. But the horse is also supposed to go in the direction you indicate. It is supposed to trot and gallop when you ask it to and stop on your command. To do this, the beginner learns the basic riding skills.

Maybe you want to become a successful show jumper. If you are really good, you can ride the best horses in dressage and show jumping. You start for the national team and become World Champion or Olympic Champion. Maybe you even become a professional equestrian. Your victories at big horse shows will make you famous, and you will earn a lot of money.

What are your goals? Why do you want to learn horseback riding?

With what can I reach my goals?

Now you'll ask what you can do to get better. What you can do to get a better feel for horses, to achieve a better seat on horseback and to be able to guide the horse according to your wishes. In any case, you should be at the barn as often as possible, take care of a horse, groom it and feed it. Get acquainted with the horses.

Your riding instructor will explain all of the important techniques to you step by step and let you practice. You'll certainly have fun with that. Occasionally, some of the exercises may seem boring or strenuous. Hang in there, because they help you get a little closer to your goal.

How can I reach my goal?

The more diligently and the more often you practice, the better you will get. You practice something until you've got it. Once you're satisfied, it's time for the next step. Then it gets a little more difficult and laborious again. But if you practice persistently, you will get there, too, without difficulties. One after another, you will learn the techniques you need to become a good and confident rider.

If you had to miss practice for an extended period of time due to illness or vacation, you will notice that you have slipped a little. You could say that you've gotten out of practice. Now it's time to catch up!

Try to read and learn as much as you can about horses, their care, the keeping of horses, etc. Observe horses and how experienced riders handle them.

Goals for the horse

What about our goals?

Of course, no horse will sit in its stall at night writing down practice goals for the following day. It won't dream about being World Champion either! They are, after all, animals. They act on their innate instincts and on emotion.

"If I do well in this exercise, I'll get a treat!"
Or: "If I go fast now, I'll get back to my stall, my feeder, and the other horses sooner."

But horses also need goals for the practice sessions. Although these are their natural movements, there still is a lot they have to learn. We humans do the thinking and planning for them. Soon after the birth of a foal, horse experts can assess what its capabilities will be and how well it might perform some day. Now the horse must also learn step by step. And someone who is patient will have lots of fun with the horse while reaching mutual goals together.

Every horse is different. It is nice if you have the opportunity to work with the same horse for a longer period of time.

Look at this picture. What do you think of it? Write down your thoughts here.

. . . . .5 FIT AND HEALTHY

Most people who are involved in a sport want to have fun and be successful. But another important goal is keeping your body fit and healthy.

Learning to eat right

People who play sports and spend a lot of time outdoors use up more energy than a couch potato does. That's why food always tastes best after practices; you are hungry and thirsty and need to replenish your energy supply.

Oh, here is someone who is really hungry and thirsty! He would like to eat and drink everything all at once.

What would you suggest he do? Cross out the things you think are not very healthy!

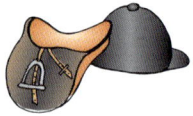

Almost all children love to eat candy bars, chips, fries and pizza. Of course, that's not exactly athlete's food, especially if you eat these things often and in large quantities. These foods contain too much fat.

A better meal for athletes is whole grain bread with cheese, fruit and yogurt. There are lots of foods that are healthy and taste good. Try to have a varied diet and eat in moderation. You don't want to get too heavy for your horse!

If you sweat, you need to drink regularly

When you sweat, you lose a lot of fluids that you need to replenish by drinking sufficiently. Water, juice mixes (fruit juice mixed with water), or tea (even sweetened with honey) are best for quenching your thirst. Pure juice or sodas are not suitable as liquid replacements. They contain too much sugar.

When you are thirsty and getting a drink, make sure you don't drink too hastily. It is better to take small sips more frequently. Be careful not to overfill your stomach, because you will have a hard time moving around.

Oh boy! My stomach is so full! And I was just really thirsty.

A horse also should not drink too hastily after practicing! You can avoid that by leaving the bit in its mouth.

Hello, Doc!

You should cheerfully say, "Hello, Doc!" to your doctor because as an athlete you usually feel totally fit. Even if you are not sick, you need to visit your doctor. Tell him you are learning horseback riding. He or she will examine you, look at your back and tell you if you can ride without any concerns.

Have your vaccination record updated and get some nutritional tips.

A successful day begins with a good start in the morning!

Some tips from Max:

Go to bed on time, and get plenty of sleep!

Look forward to the new day.

Stretch after getting up. How about some morning calisthenics? You'll find some exercises on the next page.

After washing, a cold shower is just the thing. It's refreshing and toughens you up.

Whole grain bread, cereal, milk, yogurt, and fruit are part of a good and healthy breakfast.

Don't forget to brush your teeth after you eat.

Stand on your toes and reach up with your arms like you are trying to pick an apple off a tree.

Then suddenly collapse and make yourself really small.

Here are some exercises you can do as part of your morning calisthenics. Surely you'll think of some more.

Lie down flat on your back and lift your pelvis. Hold this position for a moment.

Twist your hips from side to side.

Bend to the right.

Bend to the left.

Do these exercises slowly and hold each position for approximately ten seconds (count to ten).

Open the window to allow fresh air into the room. Don't forget to breathe regularly.

On this photo you can see two mares with their foals.

Have you ever had a chance to see how little foals always find their own mommy amongst all of the other horses and are nursed by her?

· · · · · · · · · · · · · · · · · ·6 THE HORSE – A RIDER'S PARTNER AND FRIEND

You are so big! And sooo beautiful …!

When people began to ride horses they first had to get to know the wild horses and tame them. They discovered many characteristics and behavior patterns shared by all horses. These are innate and have been preserved to this day.

Every rider and beginning rider should know the characteristics of horses. Only then can he connect with his horse and keep and take care of it properly. If you know how and why a horse reacts a certain way in some situations, you can lead it more easily and understand its behavior patterns. They do certain things out of instinct and not because they want to upset you.

The horse is a herd animal

No horse likes to be alone. Horses are used to living with a herd and therefore always seek contact with other horses. "Horsey friends" like standing close together. They like to touch and affectionately nibble on each other. When you are alone with your horse in the riding arena or on the trail, you have to gently get him used to the separation. Always let him know you are there. Whenever you meet up with other horses on the trail, your horse will start speeding up to catch up with the other members of its species.

This is how you can use this peculiarity to your advantage:

For instance, if your horse doesn't want to enter a new riding arena or go through water, you can ask a more experienced horse to lead the way. Your horse will be sure to follow.

Horses have a pecking order

Every herd has a strict pecking order. It is established by the horses. Once the pecking order has been established, the lead stallion takes over and issues orders to the animals in his herd. Whatever he does, all the other horses do, too. Aside from the lead stallion there is a lead mare and other important animals. If a new horse comes into the herd or two unfamiliar horses meet up, the battle for the pecking order begins immediately.

This is how you can use this peculiarity to your advantage:

To your horse, you are the highest ranking animal, the "lead stallion." Show the horse calmly and with determination what he needs to do. Don't go in for any little games or power struggles!

Horses are very cautious and fearful

Horses flee from danger to protect and save themselves. They react according to how big they perceive the danger to be. If it is nothing out of the ordinary, some horses will jerk because they are startled. Or they stand still and take a closer look. If it looks a little more dangerous they jump sideways, whereby they may lose a rider. When horses are really frightened they run off. When they are in a huge panic they don't hear or see anything. That's when it may even happen that the rider gets run over.

This is how you handle this peculiarity:

If you ever get thrown off or run over by a frightened horse, don't be angry at him and punish him. He didn't intend to hurt you. You should familiarize your horse with a new situation or a strange object calmly, and with patience and determination

Horses need lots of exercise

Horses living in the wild moved around a lot. They used to be on the move as much as twenty hours a day searching for food and drinking water. Often they only slept standing up. Besides, their stomach is designed in such a way that it constantly wants to ingest and digest food.

This is how you handle this peculiarity:

Your horse needs lots of exercise for proper development. Make sure that it doesn't spend the better part of the day in a stall. Let it out often into a pasture, let it graze and take it out on trail rides.

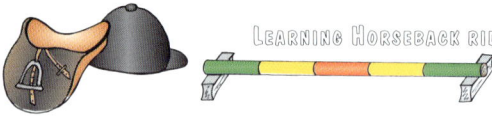

Parts of the Horse

Anyone working with horses should quickly learn the proper names for the parts of a horse's body. It is a little embarrassing to call things by the wrong name. But it's even worse if you don't understand what the riding instructor or other riders are talking about.

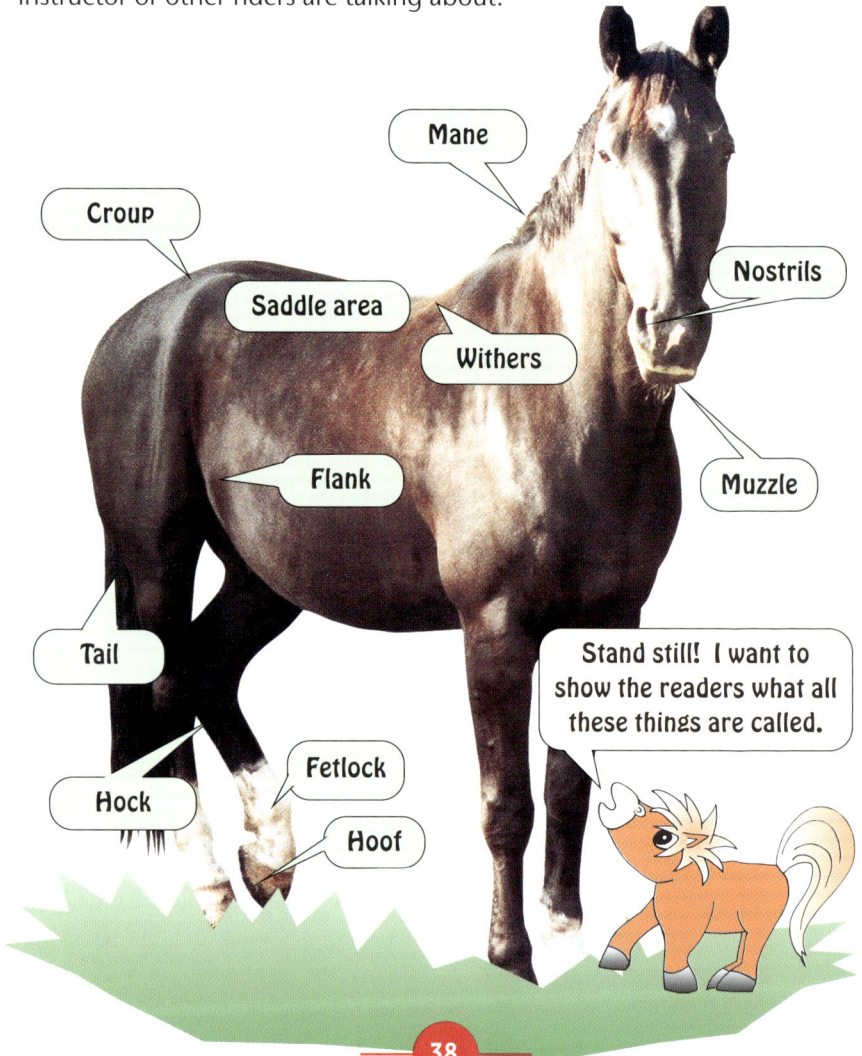

Mane

Croup

Saddle area

Withers

Nostrils

Flank

Muzzle

Tail

Stand still! I want to show the readers what all these things are called.

Fetlock

Hock

Hoof

When friends, parents, grandparents or siblings ask you about the correct names for the parts of the body, how do you answer them?

Enter your answers in the crossword puzzle!

1. Do horses eat with their mouth? What is the correct name?

2. What do you call the area from the highest point on a horse's hindquarters to the tail? You shouldn't get your foot caught there when you mount or dismount.

3. What do you call the pretty hair on the horse's neck?

4. When horses walk by it makes such a clattering sound. What do they have on their hoofs?

5. What do you call their bangs?

6. I sometimes put my hair in a ponytail? Do horses have those, too?

7. Horses are measured in "hands". Where is the highest point for that?

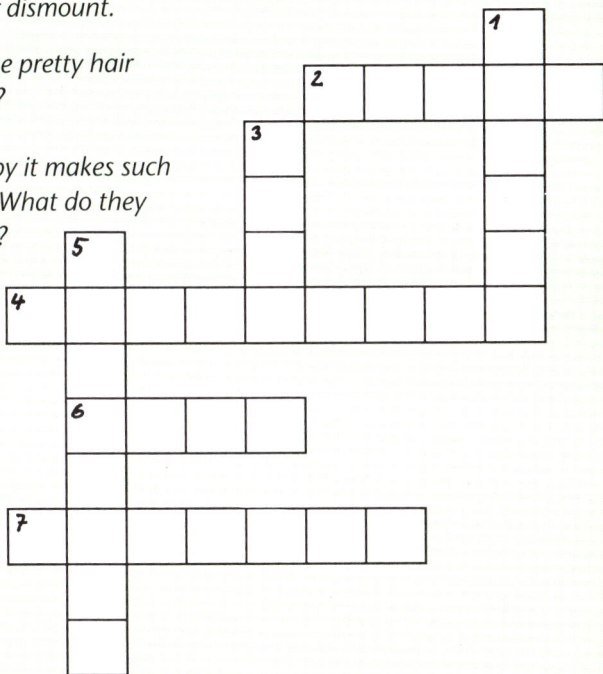

Can you tell what is going on with me?

Am I hungry?

Am I frightened or startled?

Do I like you or not?

Am I panicked?

Maybe I'm just trying to make you think, because no horse looks like I do!

Horse language

Of course horses don't use words like we do. They have other means of communicating with each other, or to tell you what they want and how they are feeling.

Sometimes you hear them making these noises. Do you know what they mean? Observe and listen to the horses and draw connecting lines. There are also multiple meanings.

Neighing •

Blowing breath •

Snorting •

Squealing •

• Feeling good
• Excitement
• Greeting
• Rejection
• Joy
• Threat

Horses don't usually roar loudly or chatter like other animals. They are pretty quiet. They can express themselves with the way they hold their head, with their ears, their eyes, and their nostrils.

Have you observed these forms of expression in horses? The next time you notice them, mark the appropriate box.

The ears are pricked. The horse is looking intently off into the distance.

One ear is turned back because it hears something back there. It is probably listening to its rider.

The head is extended forward, the nostrils are flared, and the ears are back. Watch out! This horse is pretty angry!

This expression is called "flehming." Something must smell interesting. But be aware: it can also indicate pain from colic.

Learn to understand the "horse language." If you're not real sure, ask your riding instructor or an experienced rider.

Learn to "talk" to horses. Your horse can read your tone of voice and your body language.

1

2

3

4

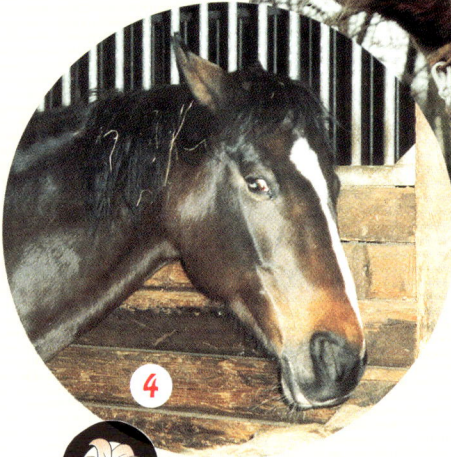

5

How would you assess the horses in these photos?

Horse tack

As a beginning rider, you won't have to take care of the horse tack right away. The riding instructor makes sure that everything is there and in good condition. He will lift the heavy saddle onto the horse's back and he will put the bridle on large horses.

But you should still be interested in it right from the start. Ask what the various parts of the saddle and bridle are called and watch when horses are being tacked up. Maybe you'll even get to help.

Which pieces of horse tack do you know already? Write them down here and draw them on the horse!

The gaits

When a human baby is born, it just lies there for a long time. Gradually, it begins to turn over, crawl, and after about one year, it starts to walk. The first steps are very shaky and the child falls down often.

It is very different with little foals. Shortly after birth, they stand up and take their first steps. The very next day, they try to take small leaps and gallop after their mother.

Horses don't need to learn the three *basic gaits* from their horse parents or from us humans. These are inborn. They already know how to *walk*, *trot*, and *canter* from birth. They also already know how to get over obstacles.

Some horse breeds have additional gaits. Write down the ones you know here!

The walk

The walk is the slowest of the horse's gaits. All four legs move evenly one after another. On a hard surface, you can clearly hear the four hoofs hit the ground. What you hear is a four-count beat.

Left rear – left front – right rear – right front
tap – tap – tap – tap

The trot

The trot is a little faster than the walk. Sometimes it almost seems like the horse is floating above the ground. As you can see in the illustration, two legs always move simultaneously: left front and right rear, then right front and left rear. You can hear a *two-count beat.*

short floating phase   short floating phase   short floating phase

tap – tap – tap – tap

The canter

The horse moves fastest in a canter. Two legs always move simultaneously and two legs move in succession. You can hear a three-count beat. The illustration shows a gallop on the left lead.

tap – tap (2 legged support) – tap (1 legged support)   floating phase

The hoofs in the colored boxes touch the ground, and the other hoofs are in the air. The tap is when we can hear hoofs hitting the ground.

Look at the illustrations on page 45 and watch the horses in the pasture and in the riding arena.

Now, try to imitate the step sequence with your fingers.

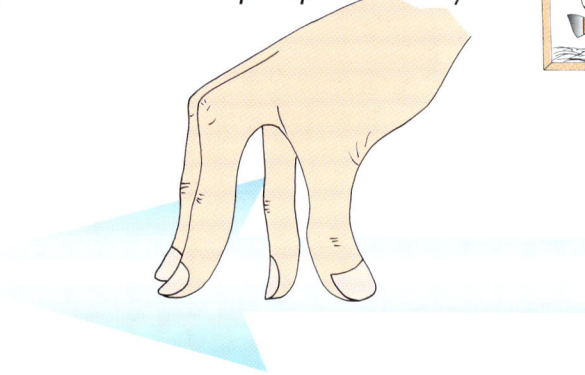

Have you tried the different gaits yet? Mark them here and add the date.

	On the lunge line	Alone
Walk		
Trot		
Canter		

Every horse is different

There are big, small, stout, fast, brown, black, spotted, quiet, and spirited horses. Some are easy to lead and others are particularly strong-willed and require a strict "boss."

By observing and handling horses, you will soon discover their differences. That is very important if you are going to be partners and you will be working with the horse.

Do I need a horse of my own?

That would be the greatest: a horse of your own! Is it necessary and even possible? Of course you don't ask yourself that question in the beginning, but only when you know that you will be riding for a long time and will want to spend a lot of time doing it.

A horse is expensive to buy, keep, and feed. And you have to pay for occasional visits by the veterinarian and the farrier. In addition, it requires lots of care and exercise. If you're not sure, think about sharing a horse.

Together with your parents, make a list of all the pros and cons of owning your own horse.

Pros	Cons

Do you have a favorite horse?

Why do you like this particular horse so much? Describe what it looks like and its qualities. Add a photo.

Name:

. . . . .7 THE RIDER

A rider's major responsibility

Without a horse, there is no rider!
That is why we first want to talk about the special relationship between the rider and his horse.

The horse hasn't lived in its natural environment for a long time. The wild herds living on the open range are almost all gone. Horses also no longer have the opportunity to search for food on their own. They are dependent on us humans. We must take care of them.

Most of the time, a rider has a favorite horse. You probably do, too. Nevertheless, every horse needs to be respected, looked after, and cared for. It doesn't matter what a horse looks like, how old it is, or how well it performs. We look after all of those that are under our care.

What's most important is a horse's health and wellbeing. Even if we have our sights on a big goal and feel perfectly fit ourselves, that's not enough. The horse must also be willing and capable to perform. We must be considerate if it needs rest or is ill. Watch your horse carefully because it can not tell you when something hurts. You will only know by observing untypical and odd behavior.

Anyone who handles horses, keeps them, takes care of them and works with them must know these things. This includes proper nutrition, accommodations appropriate to the species, physical and medical care. Learn a lot about horses and horseback riding.

Ooh, nice!! I hope it's Christmas soon!

The equipment

Have you ever looked in the window of a tack shop in total amazement, like our little Max? There is everything a rider's heart could desire and just a little bit more.

But don't worry! You don't have to come to your first riding lessons dressed like you are going to a horse show. Before you have someone buy you expensive things, try horseback riding first to make sure you'll actually enjoy it and will stick with it for some time. You can always get those fancy things later.

What you need for learning to ride

To make sure you learn to ride safely and well protected, you need to keep in mind some things about your clothing. Here, we have listed the most important items.

Riding helmet

Practical top

Gloves

Comfortable, form-fitting pants

Boots

The riding helmet

It could happen that you fall off your horse. Maybe you don't have a good seat when you jump or your horse suddenly startles and throws you off. But it isn't that bad. Your riding instructor will explain how to catch yourself when you fall, and the riding helmet will protect you from head injuries.

A proper riding helmet has a three- or four-prong fastener and fits firmly on your head. If it slides around, it can't give you proper protection. If you don't yet own your own helmet, ask at the barn to see if you can borrow one. Some riding instructors also permit you to wear a good bicycling or inline skating helmet in the beginning.

If you have long hair, tie it back.

Never get on a horse without wearing your helmet! Get used to wearing a helmet right from the start, even if you should see other riders not doing so. Your riding instructor will also make sure that you wear one.

What do you have on your head?

I couldn't find my riding helmet!

What do you think of that?

The top

The show jumpers look so good in their black or red coats! But those are not suitable for practicing. Wear a warm, comfortable jacket or a sweater for protection from wind and rain. These clothes should not be too baggy because the riding instructor won't be able to observe your form. They also shouldn't be too long so you won't sit on them.

The gloves

When you hold the reins tightly in your hands, you can sometimes get blisters on your palms. Those hurt! To avoid that, wear gloves so you can hold the reins tightly and protect your hands. Those nice white gloves look neat but they are really just for shows.

The pants

The pants should fit comfortably and never pinch or chafe, or wrinkle on the inside. Choose a comfortable pair of pants, form-fitting exercise pants, or leggings. Jeans aren't flexible enough, they are often too tight and the inseams rub. If you are going to stick with horseback riding, a special pair of riding pants is probably the first piece of clothing you should ask for.

The boots

What's most important about the boots is:

- They should have heels so your feet won't slip through the stirrups.
- The tread should not be too heavy so you don't get caught in the stirrups if you fall off.
- They need to cover your ankles so the stirrups won't injure them.

If you have found some winter boots, rubber riding boots or something similar, those should be fine for a start. You can buy those nice leather boots later. Maybe you'll even want to wait until your feet stop growing every year.

As a horse lover, you'll probably want to draw horses, too. But that's pretty difficult! How about a cartoon horse?

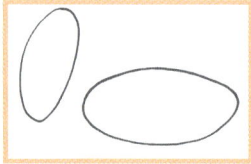

Here is room for your own attempt!

A rider has to be fit

Did you maybe think that horseback riding is when the horse moves and the rider just sits on its back? That poor horse would have to carry around a stiff, inflexible and awkward person like a sack of potatoes. Do you want your horse to make nice, powerful and elegant movements? Then you need to be fit and athletic, too. It is the only way horse and rider can become one and give a good athletic performance.

Prepare for riding by strengthening your muscles, improving your flexibility and working on your endurance. You will need a flexible back, good abdominal muscles, and strong thighs and arms.

☐ Bicycling
☐ Running
☐ Dancing
☐ Ping-pong
☐ Soccer
☐ Gymnastics
☐ Skiing
☐ Swimming
☐ Volleyball
☐ Inline skating

Many other sports are good for supplemental training and keeping fit.

☐ _____

Mark the sports you enjoy doing. Is your favorite sport not listed? Add it to the list.

☐ _____

☐ _____

We have listed some exercises on the following pages. Do these to strengthen your riding muscles and to increase your flexibility. You can do them at home or together with your riding buddies. Don't forget to warm up!

Exercises for strengthening your back muscles

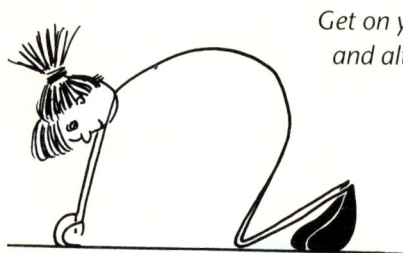

Get on your knees and alternately

make a cat back...

and a donkey back.

Your rear is at your heels. Now push forward staying nice and low, then come back up to a cat back and push your rear back to your heels.

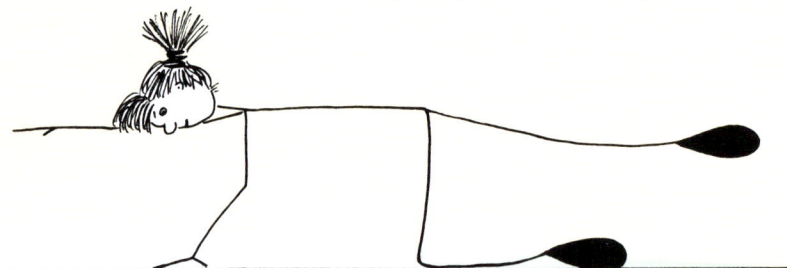

Alternately extend your arms forward and your legs back. Now try doing them together: right arm and left leg, then left arm and right leg. Don't forget to breathe!

... and increasing flexibility

Lie on your stomach and lift your trunk slightly.

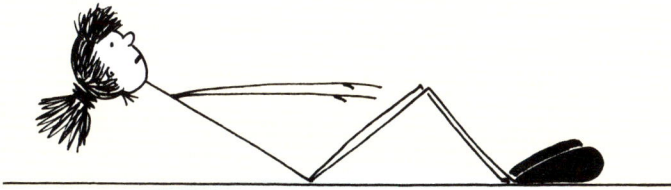

Sit ups: lie on your back, bend your knees, and lift your trunk. Can you feel your abdominal muscles?

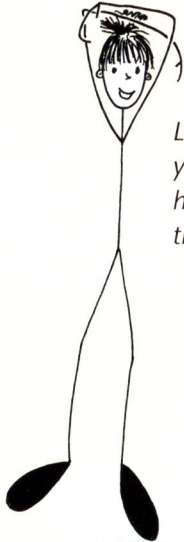

Lift your arms behind your head; with one hand grip the elbow of the other arm and pull!

One hand comes from the top and the other from the bottom. Can the tips of your fingers touch behind your back?

Don't forget to breathe regularly!

Take a look at these riders. Can you see what's wrong with their attire?

1

2

3

Are all of the horses identical? No, only two horses are really twins. Which ones are they?

1 2 3 4

5 6 7 8

9 10 11 12

.........8 BASIC HORSEMANSHIP

You watched horses in the pasture and in the barn. Maybe you even got to pet and feed them. If you want to be able to handle them properly and ride them, there are some important things you need to learn right from the start.

Riding instructors also refer to this as: learning *basic horsemanship*.

That includes:

Grooming

Leading

Sitting

Feeding

Using aids

Maybe you thought that after your first riding lesson you would already be galloping through a field like the cowboys and Indians in the movies? But it doesn't work that fast, even with the best horse. At first, there are many riding lessons on the lunge line in the arena. If you keep at it and work hard, you'll soon get to go on a trail ride.

Leading

Some people have great respect for horses or are even a little afraid of them. Whenever they are near horses, they keep their distance and don't dare to move. That is understandable because horses are large animals with a will of their own. You can't turn off their engine and pull the brake to make them stop like a car.

People have to acquire a feel for the behavior of horses and learn to handle them.

This is what's important:

- The horse trusts you.
- The horse respects you.
- The horse allows you to lead him.

What is your technique for befriending a strange horse? What kinds of tips did you get from your riding instructor?

How to gain a horse's trust

If you don't want to make any mistakes during your first encounter with a horse, try to put yourself in the horse's place. A horse has excellent eyes and ears and notices the slightest movement. Approach the horse in a friendly manner and with a calm voice. Call it by name. Remember that its eyes are at the side of its head and it can't see you if you stand right in front of its nose. Don't startle the horse by suddenly popping up, yelling, or making wild movements.

Horses like being touched and stroked. Pet it and scratch its coat. If you bring your horse a treat, it will know that you like it.

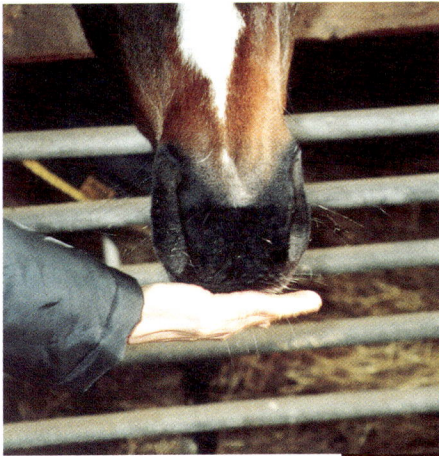

Beware:
Only feed with an open hand!

Hold your thumb against your hand! Or else the horse may think your finger is something to nibble on!

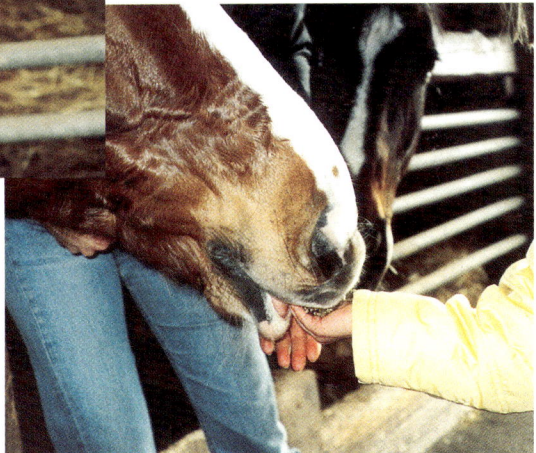

Gaining a horse's respect

As you already know, the horse is a herd animal. Every herd has a lead stallion that all of the other horses follow and are subordinate to. Don't get involved in any power struggles. To the horse, you should be the lead stallion and not the other way around. You are in charge and make the rules.

Even if you love your horse a bunch and want to just cuddle it all day, you need to be the boss! If you are too playful and silly, your horse will no longer respect you as the "lead stallion" and will want to take charge himself. Never let it get to a point where the horse is bossing you.

- Caresses are only intended as friendly gestures and rewards.
- When a horse is defiant, it needs to be reprimanded with a firm voice or even a slap. Your slap can be a little harder because horses are not as sensitive as we are.

This is taking it a little too far. Max is a stuffed animal and can stay in bed, but a real horse needs to sleep in its stall.

How to lead a horse

You lead your horse from the stall to the grooming spot or the pasture. For that, you use a rope that is hooked to the halter.

Here the rope is attached at the bottom center. When you pull down, the halter puts pressure on the nasal bone. When you pull to the side, the halter puts pressure on the opposite side.

If the rope is attached at the side of the halter, you can assert more pressure to stubborn horses. When you pull on the side, the halter shifts slightly over the horse's eye. The horse finds this unpleasant and you achieve your goal more quickly.

If the rope is attached at the side, you can also loop it under the chin and pull it through the ring on the other side. Now, when you pull, the halter gets a little tighter and puts pressure on the entire nasal bone.

Instead of running the rope under the chin, you can also run it through the mouth. For training purposes, some horses require a little more painful pressure.

Don't be afraid that you will hurt your horse. You only pull briefly to get the horse's attention. Wait a moment to see if it understood your signal. If not, you will need to be more insistent. Then immediately relax the rope again.

63

As you already know, there are many reasons why your horse may startle and suddenly jerk. In doing so, it will pull very hard on the rope. Of course you want to hold on to your horse, but not at any cost.

Hold the rope so you can release it if there is too much pressure.

If you wind the rope around your hand, you will get caught and the rope will hurt you as it constricts.

This is how you lead

When you lead your horse, you walk on the left side. The horse's head should be close to you so you can observe the horse as you lead it. This way you will be able to see if the horse is content or if it hears something unsettling.

Don't yank on the rope. As you lead practice having your horse walk in your direction after just a gentle tug.

But you have to assert yourself! When necessary, use more force.

When another horse is in the way

Occasionally it happens that you, or you and your horse, can't go down a barn aisle or a narrow passage because another horse is in the way.

How can you get that horse to step aside?

Calmly approach the horse and talk to it in a friendly manner until it acknowledges your presence. Tell him earnestly that he needs to move out of the way. At the same time, tap the horse on his flank. If it doesn't work the first time, try it again. You can also push the horse in the desired direction.

If you're not sure or your approach isn't working, ask someone to help you. Get your riding instructor or another experienced rider.

If you have the opportunity, try out passing by. Record your attempts and successes including the dates, here. Don't overdo it! Always be alert and careful.

Attempt/Date	Did it work: Yes/No

What happens when you lead your horse past a basket filled with apples?

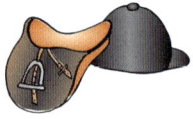

Grooming

Part of a rider's responsibility is the grooming of his horse. Most people do it themselves because it is a good way to interact with the horse and gain his trust.

Natural personal hygiene

Horses love to roll. It doesn't matter if it's in grass, straw, dust or sand, mud or snow. Once they have found a suitable spot, they lie down with delight, roll their bodies, and rub their heads and necks. It makes them feel great and at the same time, they are doing something to care for their coats.

Horses like contact with other horses and with people. They enjoy being stroked and petted. It's like a nice massage. But just like us humans, not all horses are alike. Find out what your horse likes, where it doesn't like to be touched when you groom it, and where it might even be ticklish.

We use the horses' delight in touching, rubbing, scrubbing and massaging to our advantage when we groom them.

The horse's coat

Horses need their coat as you need your clothing. It protects them from cold, heat, rain and wind. And like you have your summer and winter clothes the horse grows a summer coat, and during the cold winter it has a thick, fuzzy winter coat. It needs it if it doesn't want to freeze out in the pasture.

Some riders who work their horses during the winter want to prevent that thick winter coat from growing. It makes the horses sweat too heavily and they have to be rubbed dry much longer. So they put blankets on their horses' backs. It keeps the horses from getting so cold and their coats don't grow as thick.

Why we groom horses

Our horses no longer live in their natural environment. They walk on rocky surfaces and on streets. They no longer have lots of contact with their fellow horses to rub and nibble on each other. Besides, carrying a saddle was not something nature intended them to do. The horses live with us, and they need us.

We groom horses,

- so there is no dirt on the saddle area that may rub under the saddle.
- so there are no rocks under the hoofs that could hurt as they walk.
- because grooming is like a good massage that improves circulation.
- because we like to take care of our horses, and it is a good way to bond.

The best place for grooming

To groom your horse, find a quiet spot where you have plenty of room for your horse and where there won't be any disruptions. The best places are outside or in the barn aisle. A stall is not as good because dirt and hair will remain in the stall and may be eaten along with the hay.

Grooming Utensils

Do you use more than these? Add your own drawings. Remember that it is best for each horse to have his own grooming utensils. This helps to prevent the spread of diseases. You don't want to share your toothbrush with your whole family either!

This is how you groom

Use the **rubber curry brush** to rough up the coat with circular strokes. This loosens the dirt and dust and is also a great massage. You can rub hard along the muscles. But be gentle along bones. Rubbing too hard with the stiff curry brush can hurt the horse. You can also use a **rubber curry glove with massage knobs** on those areas.

The **body brush** is much softer. You use it to smooth down the coat, brushing in the direction the hair grows. This gets the dust out of the coat and makes it look nice and smooth. Every so often, run the body brush through the curry brush to get the dirt out.

If there is any hard or sticky dirt left on the legs, you can use a **coarse scrubbing brush** to remove it.

The **curry comb** is used for the mane. You can also use it to thin out an overly thick mane. This is called pulling the mane. But don't comb the tail. Tail hair can get pulled out easily causing the tail to get thinner and thinner. You can pick pieces of hay and dirt out by hand. Use your fingers to gently sort the tail hair.

Small stones tend to always get lodged in the hoofs. These hurt the horse as it walks. You use a **hoof pick** to dislodge the stones from the hoofs.

Stones and asphalt really wear down the hoofs. That is why special hoof care is necessary. Brush some **hoof conditioner** on the clean hoofs. This promotes hoof growth and looks nice. Use the conditioner particularly along the coronet band (where the hair starts) because that is where the hoof grows and where good care is most critical.

Use the **sponge** to clean the head, the saddle area, and any other sticky places.

LEARNING HORSEBACK RIDING

Look for grooming utensils horizontally, vertically, or diagonally. You will find more items than the ones we listed on the previous pages.

A	D	G	A	S	M	M	V	A	S	M	P	C	S
E	Q	F	L	Y	S	P	R	A	Y	A	E	Z	H
H	O	O	F	P	I	C	K	U	I	U	T	O	E
D	C	O	H	J	A	P	I	L	W	O	A	L	D
A	L	C	N	E	R	E	S	P	A	G	C	V	D
S	I	K	A	J	V	N	S	I	M	S	K	F	I
I	P	C	U	R	R	Y	C	O	M	B	B	L	N
S	P	O	G	J	B	U	I	S	T	E	O	Y	G
G	E	M	N	R	E	R	S	E	F	J	X	M	B
E	R	O	T	G	M	S	S	L	R	S	F	A	L
A	S	T	T	F	E	T	O	Q	R	A	U	S	A
O	L	U	G	C	S	E	R	M	E	R	G	K	D
B	O	D	Y	B	R	U	S	H	M	D	A	Z	E

Did you work up a sweat grooming your horse? That's good! Now you're already halfway warmed up for your lesson.

70

Properly tying a horse

When you want to groom a horse, you lead it to a suitable spot and tie it there. You wouldn't want it to just walk off in the middle of your grooming session because it sees something interesting.

These horses have a problem. What was not done correctly when they were tied? Correct the drawing by showing how the rope is tied properly!

When you want to tie your horse for grooming, find a safe place and something solid to tie it to. Usually there are grooming areas outside the stalls with special rings or cross ties. Attach the rope securely by tying a knot. However, if you tie a regular knot, the rope will be attached, but if the horse suddenly jerks, the knot gets pulled so tight that you won't be able to undo it and the rope will have to be cut off. If a dangerous situation should occur, you won't be able to release the rope quickly enough. That is why horse handlers use a special *"safety knot"*. It is very secure but can also be released quickly and easily.

Just like sailors have their special sailor's knots, horse handlers and riders know at least one safety knot for tying horses. Have someone show you how to tie different knots and practice them.

Mounting up

If you want to ride, you first need to mount up. That isn't always easy to do because most horses are quite tall. Using a mounting aid is a more pleasant way for rider and horse. Climb up on a mounting block or a raised area, or ask someone to give you a "leg up."

But a true rider must be able to mount up without help!

This is how it's done:

You mount up from the left side. Take the reins in your left hand and hold on to the saddle. Place your left foot in the stirrup.

Grip the back of the saddle with your right hand and turn toward the saddle.

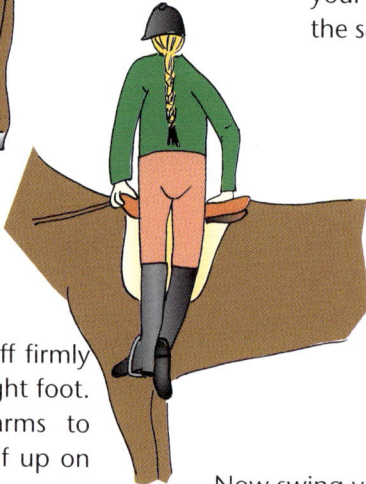

Now push off firmly with your right foot. Use both arms to push yourself up on the saddle.

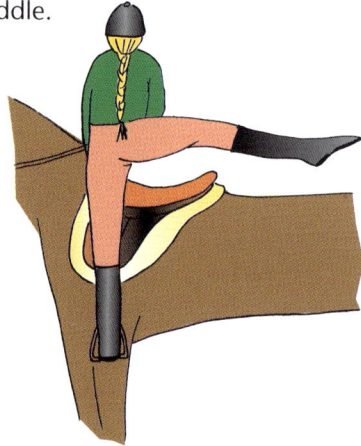

Now swing your right leg over the horse's back and gently sit down in the saddle.

To keep the saddle from sliding, ask a helper to hold down your right stirrup as you mount up.

The following are things you should pay attention to when mounting up. Which mistakes do you occasionally make? Check them off. But use a pencil so you can hopefully erase those checks again soon. If your riding instructor makes another important suggestion, add it to the list.

☐ Make sure the girth is tight. Otherwise the saddle may slide to the side when you put your weight in the stirrup.

☐ Stand at an angle to the horse.

☐ Push off hard with your right foot to gain enough momentum.

☐ Be careful not to accidentally kick your horse in the belly. It may think it's supposed to take off.

☐ Look up the horse's neck. That will help you keep your balance.

☐ Make sure you don't hang on the horse's side too long. It is uncomfortable for the horse.

☐ Be careful not to kick the horse's side as you swing your leg over. He may take that as a signal to take off, too.

☐ Sit down slowly and gently in the saddle.

☐

Sometimes you have trouble mounting up because you don't have enough momentum and get caught. In that case, just pull yourself up like a little monkey.

Maybe you have a helper who can give you a good push on your rear. Otherwise start over! All it takes is practice!

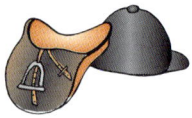

Sitting

Have you noticed how proud the riders sit on their horses? The torso is erect, the gaze directed straight ahead. The rider moves with his horse in a subtle and relaxed fashion.

The most important thing a rider needs to learn right from the start is the proper seat on a horse. The rider learns to keep his balance on the horse and to become one with the horse. Only this way can the horse move properly and can the rider exert his influence over the horse.

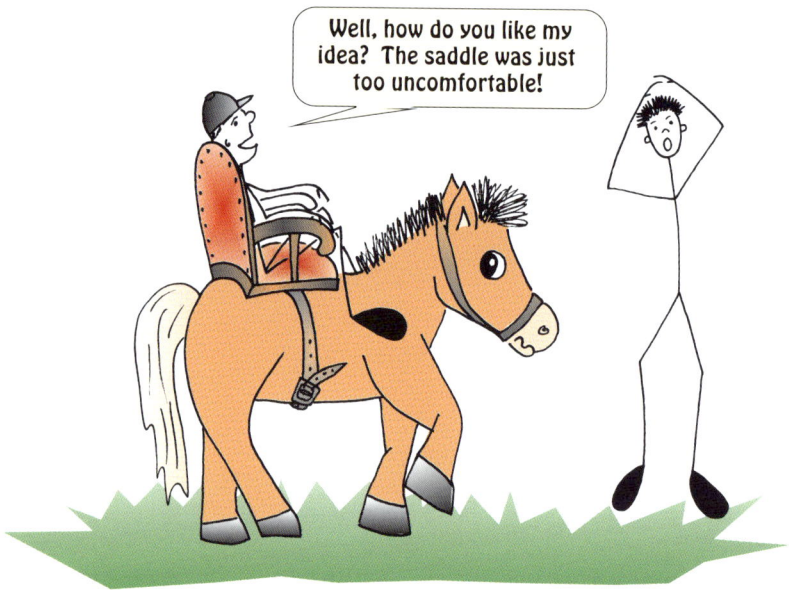

Well, how do you like my idea? The saddle was just too uncomfortable!

Just like there are different ways to ride, like dressage, jumping, and racing, there are different saddles and different ways to sit in them. The riding instructor decides which saddle and which seat you will start your lessons with.

Dressage seat

The dressage seat is the most important seat and the basis for all other seats. Rider and horse receive their training with the dressage seat.

This is what you need to pay attention to:

- ☼ The rider sits erect. Head, shoulders, hips, and heels form a straight line. The heel is the lowest point (see illustration).
- ☼ You sit in the deepest part of the saddle with your weight evenly distributed between your rear and your thighs. Your muscles are not tense.
- ☼ Your thighs are slightly rotated in so your toes don't point away from the horse. The knees rest against the saddle.
- ☼ Shoulders and arms are relaxed. The elbows are bent and the forearms rest lightly against the body. The horse's mouth, the reins, fists and elbows form a straight line (see illustration).

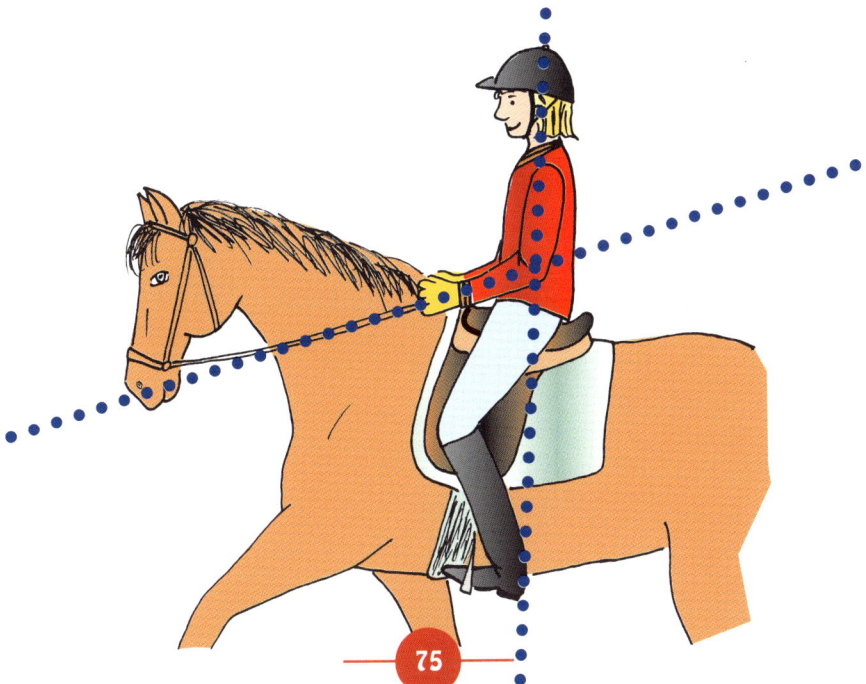

Take a close look at these illustrations. These riders do not have a good seat. What are they doing wrong? You will find the correct answers in the back of the book.

Mark the picture that shows your main problem. (But use a pencil so you can hopefully erase the mark soon!)

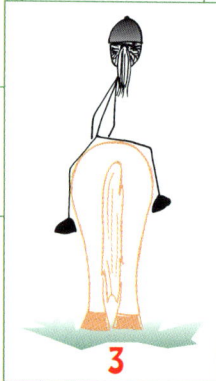

1

2

3

4

5

The jump seat

The jump seat is also called the light seat or the two-point. The rider's torso leans forward slightly and the rear doesn't push down on the horse's back as much. This makes the rider "lighter" and puts less stress on the horse's back. As the name suggests, this seat is used for jumping, but it is also suitable for trail riding.

What you need to pay attention to:

- ☼ The torso leans forward slightly. Head, shoulders, and hips form a straight line (see illustration).
- ☼ Your weight is supported primarily by your thighs, knees, and feet. Less weight is carried in the rear.
- ☼ The knees are bent more due to the shorter stirrups and are held against the horse. The lower legs lie flat against the horse.
- ☼ Due to the torso leaning forward, the reins are shorter and the arms are held in front of the body. The horse's mouth, the reins, fists, and elbows form a straight line (see illustration).

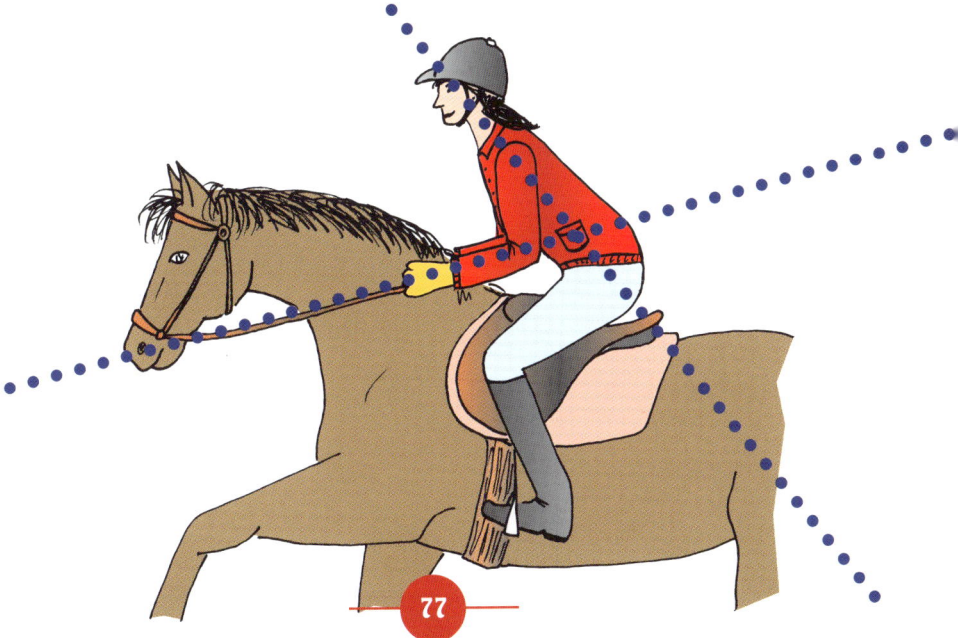

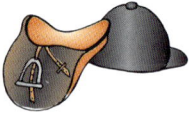

Take a close look at these illustrations. These riders do not have a good seat. What are they doing wrong?

Mark the picture that shows your main problem.

1

2

3

4

5

In order to have a good seat, you should remember the following suggestions. Which mistakes do you make occasionally? Check them off. But use a pencil so you can hopefully erase them soon. If your riding instructor has some more important suggestions, add them to the list.

The Dressage Seat

☐ Sit up straight! The torso is erect. Push the chest out. Sit proud!

☐ Hold your head straight! Don't lean forward or back!

☐ The widest part of the foot, the ball, is in the stirrup.

☐ The heel is the lowest point. The toes point up.

☐ Don't rest your fists on the horse or on your thighs.

☐ ....

☐ ....

☐ ....

☐ ....

The Jump Seat

☐ The heel is the lowest point. The toes point up.

☐ Push the foot a little farther into the stirrup.

☐ Don't hunch your back.

☐ Don't rest your fists on the horse or on your thighs.

☐ Look straight ahead. Don't look down at the horse!

☐ ....

☐ ....

☐ ....

☐ ....

For these exercises you will need a large medicine or stability ball, which are available from various manufacturers.

Sit down on the ball. Your feet are planted slightly apart and your hands rest easily on your thighs.

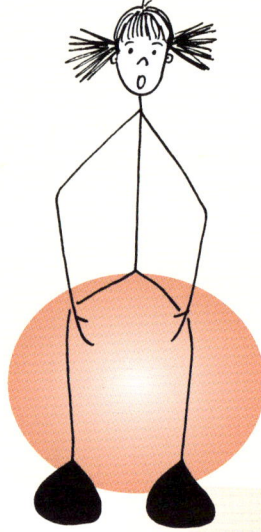

Now move the ball forward and back.

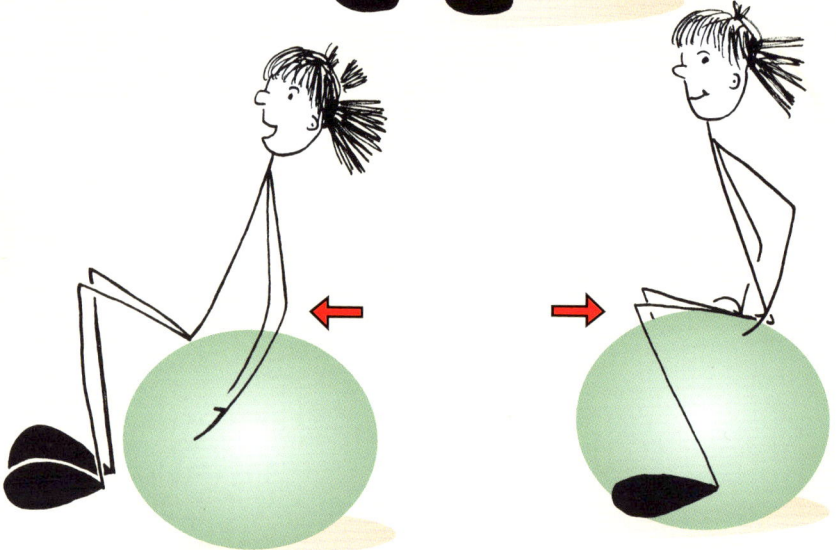

From the starting position, slide your rear first to the right and then to the left. Careful: don't fall off!

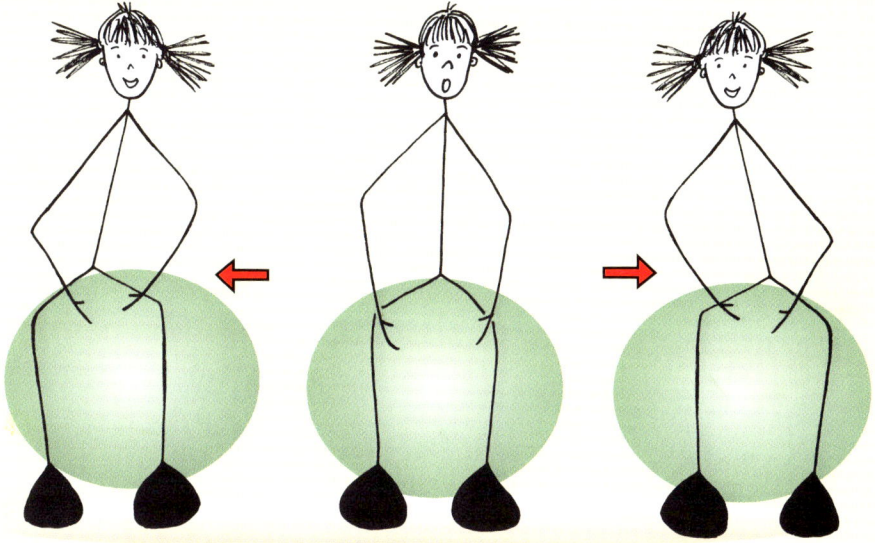

Try to imitate the riding movement on the ball. Can you do a walk, trot, trot in a two-point, or canter?

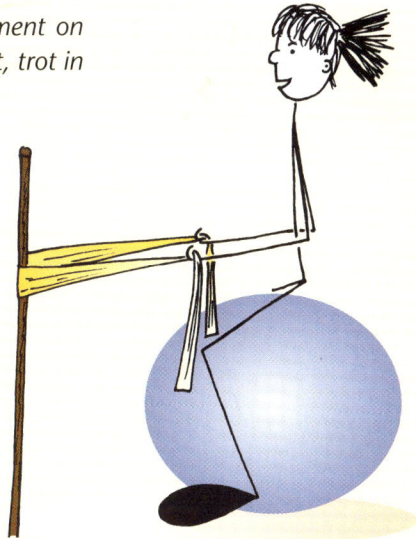

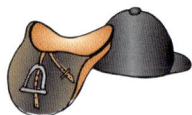 

Dismounting

Once you sit on top, you of course want to get down again, too. And you want to be able to do so as gently and skillfully as possible so rider and horse don't get injured.

This is how you dismount:

☼ Take both feet out of the stirrups. That is important in case the horse runs off as you are dismounting, so you won't get a foot caught in the stirrup.

☼ Lean forward with your torso.

☼ Swing the right leg over the saddle. Be careful not to get caught on the croup.

☼ Carefully slide down. Try to land softly.

Falling off

Every rider occasionally "dismounts" involuntarily. That means he falls off the horse!

Don't try to hold on to the horse!

When you fall off, it startles your horse, too,
and pulling on the reins may confuse it even more.

●

If you hold on to the reins and your horse runs off,
your arm may get injured from the severe pulling.

●

If your horse does run off, it's not the end of the world.
He will come back.

Your own safety comes first!

Your horse will always try not to injure you.

●

If you and your horse both fall, try to roll away from the horse.
If you fall during a trot or a gallop, you'll have enough momentum to
fall away from the horse.

●

Don't jump up immediately but stay on the ground for a moment.
Make sure everything is alright and you're not seriously injured.

Falls do happen. If it happens to you, think about what might have caused it. How can you handle it more skillfully the next time?

Cuing

The rider can give instructions to his horse by moving and applying pressure with his thighs, and by using the reins. This is called *"cuing."* It is a way for the rider to choose the gait, the tempo, and the direction of travel. When a good rider who has excellent control of his horse cues it, you barely even notice. The cues are subtle and gentle.

Pressure cuing

If you suddenly switch from a casual seat to tightening your lower back and abdominal muscles, your rear pushes deeper into the saddle. The horse feels the pressure against his back. This is called *bilateral pressure cuing.* You can spur on your horse this way, control its speed, and slow it down. Many riding instructors also call this *bracing the back*.

If you lean forward a little, you shift your weight more to your thighs and away from your rear. The horse feels less pressure. This is called *non-pressure cuing*.

When you shift your weight to just one side, you put more pressure on that side. The horse feels the increased pressure on the one side. This is *unilateral pressure cuing*. You can do this to steer your horse in a certain direction.

What is this rider doing wrong?

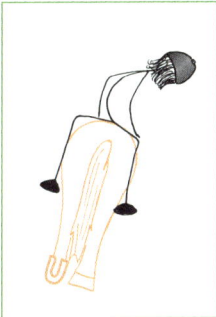

Leg cuing

While you ride, you hold your lower legs closely against the horse's sides. This way the horse can immediately feel it when you push your leg against its belly or ribs.

If you continue to push your leg into the horse's side behind the girth, you drive the horse forward. It is also called *putting a leg in*.

Cuing with reins

To be able to cue your horse with the reins, you need to learn how to properly hold the reins.

This is how you do it:

- The reins go between the pinkie and the index finger and are held with the thumb.
- The reins are not twisted and are equally long.
- The hands are held approximately 1 to 2 hand widths apart.
- The wrists are not tense.

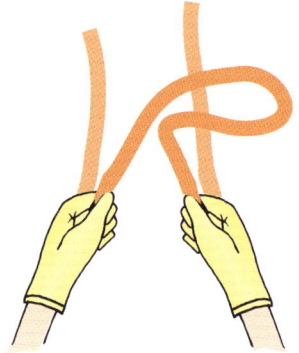

- The hands are held so the horse's mouth, the reins, and the forearms form a straight line.

If the length of the reins is not accurate, you need to change your grip. Have the other riders or your riding instructor show you how to properly do this.

What is wrong with the way these riders hold their reins?

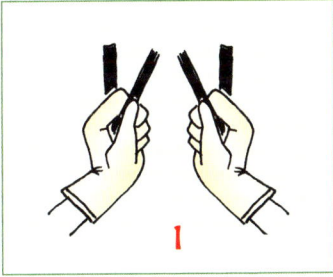

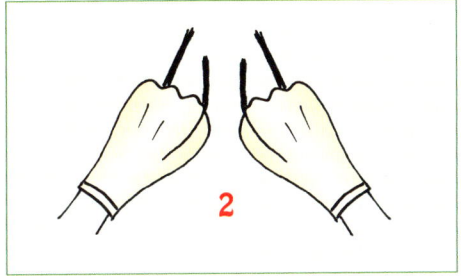

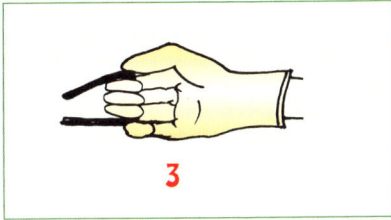

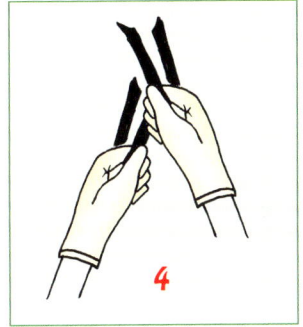

1

2

3

4

5

6

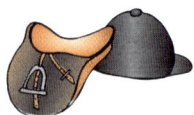

When you close your fist tightly and tilt your pinkie toward your belly button, the horse can feel a slight tug on its mouth. This is called *pulling in or checking the reins*. You can do this with both hands at the same time or separately.

When you straighten your fist out again you are *releasing the reins*. However, that doesn't mean that the reins now hang down. The contact between the rider's hand and the horse's mouth is always intact. When the hands stay in one position you are *steadying the reins*.

Cuing with the reins is always done from the wrist. Don't try to pull on the reins. That would happen if you moved your elbows back.

The check

You never use any one of the aforementioned cuing methods by itself. A check is always a combination of cuing methods. You use this, for instance, if you want your horse to slow down or even stop.

☼ With a good rider, the horse will react quickly to gentle cues.

☼ If your horse doesn't give the desired reaction, you have to repeat your cue. A little stronger if necessary.

☼ Pressure and leg cuing comes before cuing with the reins!

Don't forget that using your voice is also a necessary part of cuing. You talk to your horse to calm it, or you say: "Whoa, whoa!" You would say: "Trot!," "Canter!" to make it go, or you might click your tongue. If you say: "Whoooa!" it means you want to stop.

Write down here what you have learned.
Which cues can you use to ride your horse?

Task	Cues
Going into a canter	Move the outside thigh back a hand's breadth (or a little more) and give a squeeze at the girth with the inner thigh.
Going into a trot (transition from walk to trot)	
Stopping straight	

What are you doing? You are sitting backward on the horse!

What do you mean backward? You don't know which way I'm going!

Start keeping a practice diary for your riding lessons. You can record all the new things you learned and practiced.

Also write down any tips your riding instructor gives you.

......9 THIS IS HOW YOU PRACTICE

The first time someone gets on a horse, everything is new and strange. You sit up pretty high on a horse, it moves, and there is very little to hold on to.

Did you have an experience like the one in this drawing?

Your riding instructor will gently get you used to the horse and riding. Maybe you can sit on the horse bareback first. You can feel the animal, its strong muscles, its warmth and its movements. Your riding instructor is with you and holds the horse. Enjoy this nice new feeling of being on horseback. Relax and close your eyes and feel the swinging sensation.

On the lunge line

The lunge line is a long rope that is attached to the horse's snaffle. The riding instructor holds the other end. The horse moves in a big circle around the riding instructor.

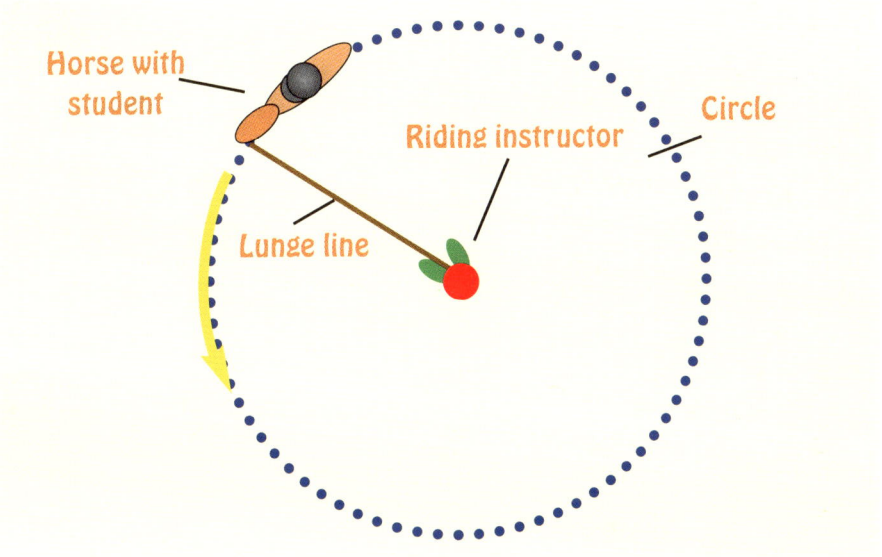

Horse with student

Circle

Riding instructor

Lunge line

Your first riding attempts are done on the lunge line. You sit on the horse, are being carried, and initially just have to worry about yourself. You feel the movements and do your first exercises on horseback. The riding instructor is in control. In the beginning, he also instructs the horse.

Practicing is done step by step. Don't be impatient! Your riding instructor will continue to make suggestions. Only when you are doing well can you tackle the next more difficult exercise.

If you are afraid, your body tenses up.
Try to feel good and relax!

There are many good exercises for limbering up on horseback. What have you tried so far? Make a check mark in the box if you've tried it. Which exercise would you like to do at your next riding lesson? Make a circle in that box for now.

	Walk	Trot	Canter
Letting go with one arm.	☐	☐	☐
Letting go with both arms.	☐	☐	☐
Letting the arms hang loosely at the side.	☐	☐	☐
Holding the arms out to the side.	☐	☐	☐
Making arm circles.	☐	☐	
Closing the eyes.	☐	☐	☐
Petting the horse on the neck.	☐	☐	☐
Petting the horse on the rump.	☐		
Slowly raising and lowering the knees.	☐		
Moving the thighs forward and back a little.	☐	☐	
Leaning forward, back, and to the side.	☐	☐	☐
....	☐	☐	☐
....	☐	☐	☐
....	☐	☐	☐

The casual seat and the formal seat

The difficult thing about sitting on a horse is that you have to continuously find your balance. It is also called finding your center of gravity. The horse is in motion and therefore your center of gravity continually changes. In addition, you should sit upright and proud, definitely not tense or stiff as a stick. That's pretty difficult and must be practiced again and again.

This is how you straighten your body:

1. Pull up your shoulders.
2. Push them back.
3. Let them drop.

A good exercise is deliberately shifting your center of gravity. To do this, you move a little farther forward, back, and to the side. It is a good way to figure out when your seat feels best. To relax, breathe deeply, stretch out and then collapse again, or tighten your muscles and then relax them.

Sitting out

When sitting out, the rider moves along with every step the horse takes. In doing so, he sits deep in the saddle. The muscles of the back and abdomen are tightened slightly and the pelvis moves supplely and easily with the movements of the horse.

Don't try to push your pelvis forward and back. Feel the movements of the horse and try to move along with it.

The posting trot

When the rider stands and sits in time with the trot, it is called a *posting trot*. You stand when the outside leg moves forward, and you sit when it moves back. How far you stand up is determined by the horse's momentum. Your heels stay down and you don't stand too far into the stirrups.

The posting trot is not as strenuous because you don't get bounced around as much, but move easily with the horse. The horse is also able to move more easily.

The first riding lesson on your own

So far you have practiced in the arena, on the lunge line and under the guidance of your riding instructor. In doing so you only had to concentrate on yourself and your horse. You practiced lots and continued to get more confident and better.

Now the time has come! This is your first riding lesson without the instructor holding the reins. Now you have to pay attention to everything yourself.

As a good lesson horse, I only react if you sit correctly and cue me properly and without hesitation!

That means first of all abiding by the riding arena rules and being considerate of other riders and other horses. In this new situation, you have to do many things simultaneously.

But what's going on? Maybe some of the things that were working just fine on the lunge line aren't working so well anymore. You are losing your good seat, you feel wobbly on the horse and your hands have a mind of their own.

But not to worry! These problems are totally normal. You need to get used to this new situation.

Small jumps

For jumping, you use the light seat or two-point as we described earlier. This takes weight off the horse's back and allows you to better move with the horse. You practice on poles lying on the ground or low cavaletti.

Once you have mastered riding over a number of cavaletti lying on the ground in a walk and a trot, you can even try jumping them in a slow canter.

The riding instructor decides the practice sequence. Some begin with the two-point and jumping to work on balance and a good seat. Others want to reinforce the dressage seat.

Some young riders may have more talent or the opportunity to practice more frequently. They will certainly achieve their goal more quickly. If you are not moving as fast, be patient and persistent. What is most important is to practice everything thoroughly and correctly. Only when you know you're ready should you move on to the next more difficult exercise.

Since you can't practice everything at once, you should have goals for each practice session. Think about what in particular you would like to practice and what specifically you need to pay attention to. Write these practice goals down.

After your riding lesson, you can show how satisfied you are by doing a little drawing:

Like this this 😊 or 🙂 *maybe this* 🙁

Date	Practice Goal	Satisfied?

These goals could be something like:
Correct hand position, good head position, torso erect, standing up to the horse, achieve good balance, setting the pace, and much more.

............10 DIFFERENT SPORTS ON AND WITH THE HORSE

Once you have learned the most important things about being around horses and horseback riding, you may soon turn to a favorite discipline.

Who is involved with horses: in sports, as an occupation or as part of one's culture? Maybe the drawings will help you! Can you think of anything else?

Dressage

Dressage is a basic requirement for all other disciplines performed on horseback. The riders also consider it calisthenics for the horse, regardless of which discipline it is being trained for.

Horse shows feature dressage tests. A rider sits erectly in the saddle and has to execute certain exercises. This is done in a rectangular area approximately 60 feet by 120 feet. There are special markers in the rectangle. The rider is graded on his or her performance.

Show jumping

Before you can begin show jumping, which is riding your horse over jumps, you must master certain dressage exercises. A jumper's seat is a little different from that of a dressage rider. It is called a *light seat* or *jump seat*. Tournaments or horse shows have jump courses, which are made up of many barriers that the rider and his horse have to clear in a specific order. The object is to make as few mistakes as possible. If two riders have the same number of mistakes, the faster time is the deciding factor. Sometimes the rider is also graded on his seat. This is called *stylistic jumping*.

Oops, we forgot the jump! Draw a nice fence in the picture.

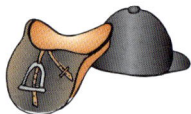

Eventing

Some equestrians call this the "crown jewel of equestrian sports." It is a so-called *triathlon for horses*. You have to pass three testing components: *dressage, jumping, and endurance*. Horse and rider must be in particularly good shape to pass all three components.

But you are not to that point yet. First you need to focus on your basic dressage training, and then you can gradually work on jumping and finally on gaining total confidence in varying outside terrain.

How would you rate your skills in the individual disciplines? Mark the various levels!

	It can do it perfectly.	
	I am satisfied with my performance.	
	I'm doing pretty well.	
	I can do it with some help.	
	I have tried it.	
	I have not tried it.	
Dressage	Jumping	Endurance

Vaulting

Many riders started out with vaulting before they ever sat in a saddle. Some equestrian clubs offer vaulting for small children but don't start them on horseback riding until several years later.

Vaulting is gymnastics on horseback, sometimes one person or multiple people at the same time. The horse does not wear a saddle but rather a girth with handles that the riders can hold on to. You don't have to wear riding pants or boots for this. Riding attire is not suited for gymnastics. Exercise tights and soft skid proof gymnastics shoes are more comfortable. You won't injure the horse with these when you stand on its back.

How do you like my pose?

You don't need to steer the horse either. It moves in a circle on the lunge line. The riding instructor holds the lunge line and chooses the horse's pace and its gait.

Trail riding

Long rides out in nature with friends or other riders are a great experience. Sometimes these rides last several hours, sometimes even several days.

You and your horse must be well conditioned to do this. You use a map to find your way. There are special accommodations where riders and horses can spend the night.

When you are out on the trail that long, you need some special gear:

- Hoof picks in case a stone gets stuck in your horse's hoof.
- Rain gear in case it suddenly begins to rain.
- Halter and lead rope so you can tie your horse during breaks.
- Flashlight in case you need to find something in the dark.
- First Aid kit in case a rider or horse gets injured.
- Compass and map so you don't get lost.

Which trail do the riders take to get from start to finish?

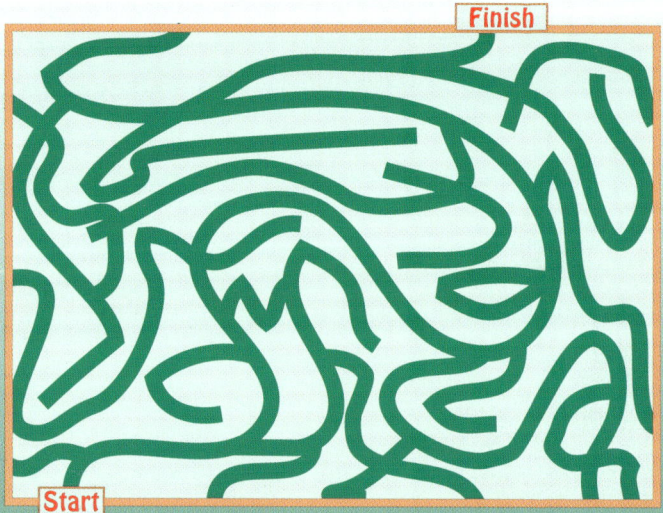

Finish

Start

Riding western

That's how the cowboys of the American West ride. They are often out for a very long time, rounding up herds of cattle. Their horses need to go long distances comfortably and effortlessly. To be able do this, they are raised and trained a certain way. These horses can be steered with minimal input from the rider. They respond well to voice commands; the rider's legs have less contact with the horse's sides and the reins are held in one hand. The western saddle is particularly comfortable. The cowboy can ride in it for a long time without getting a sore behind.

There is a special horse breed for western riding. It is called the *Quarter Horse*.

Help! I can't see a thing! Which way are we going?

Driving

The horse or pony is hitched up to a carriage or buggy with special gear called a harness. You sit down on the coach box or buggy seat and hold the long reins in your hands. You use these to steer the horse. You also give the horse voice commands.

It may look like it is just fun and games, but driving has to be properly learned! If you are untrained, you should only be in the driver's seat under the direction of an experienced driver or instructor.

.......11 KEEPING THINGS STRAIGHT

If you are a beginning rider, you always go to the riding arena with your riding instructor. He will show you the right place to mount up, get you started in the right direction, and make sure that other riders are not interfered with. You can count on that.

But at some point, you will want to go to the arena independently, without your riding instructor, to practice with your horse. That is why it is necessary that you know important rules right from the start. Observe your instructor and other riders. Memorize important rules.

Riding arena rules

Usually there is a sign with rules for using the riding arena posted at the barn. Just like with street traffic, it is important that all participants adhere to these rules. It is the only way that everyone can practice safely and without interference.

If you can't find the riding arena rules at your barn, ask someone about it. Once you've read them, you can color in the horseshoe!

Track 3

Track 2

Track 1

The most important rules

Before entering the arena, call out:
"Entrance free."
Enter only after a rider inside answers:
"Entrance free."
This also applies to leaving the arena.

•

You may not mount and dismount
on the riding track, only in the center.

•

Walking and stopping must be done
on track 2, the middle track.

•

The fast riders have "the right-away"
on track 1, the outside track.
You must yield to them to the inside.

•

When you stop, always keep a
"safe distance" of at least three paces
between you and the other horses.

•

If you want to lunge your horse,
you need to first ask the other riders.
There should be no lunging when there are
more than three riders in the arena.

Dressage figures

Anyone watching a horse show for the first time wonders what the announcements mean and how the riders know which way to go.

The arena is a rectangle, usually about 120 feet long and about 60 feet wide. There are markers in certain places which are identified by large letters. Every participant must be familiar with these markers.

You can't remember the letters? No problem!

We have a funny little saying which the rider can use to jog his memory.

A LL
K ING
E DWARD'S
H ORSES
C AN
M AKE
B IG
F ENCES

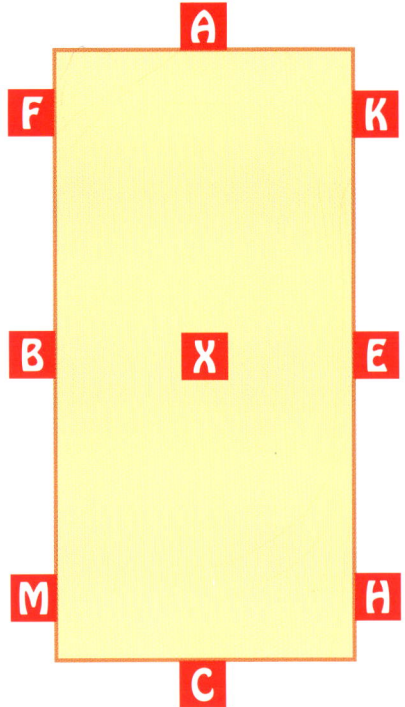

Why do you never see the letter "x" in the arena? How can you find it?

Here are a few basic dressage figures you may soon be able to ride alone, without guidance. Write down the date when you first completed them.

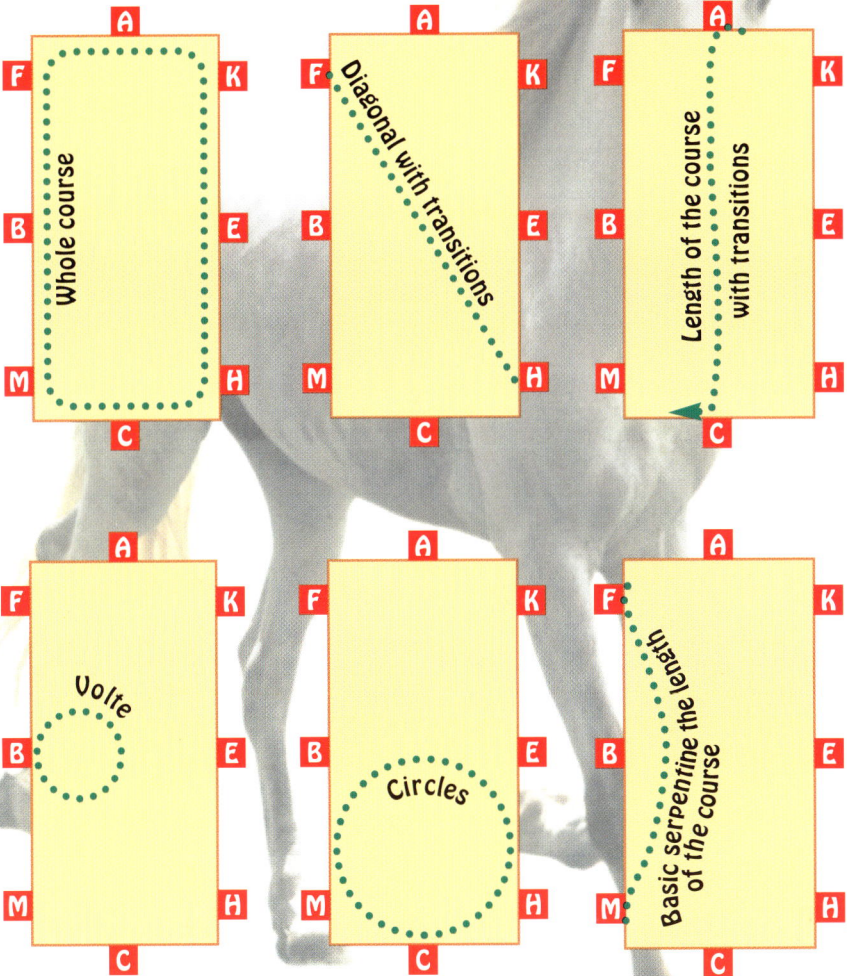

A F K B E M H C
Whole course

A F K B E M H C
Diagonal with transitions

A F K B E M H C
Length of the course with transitions

A F K B E M H C
Volte

A F K B E M H C
Circles

A F K B E M H C
Basic serpentine the length of the course

Riding on the trail

Every rider enjoys riding out in nature. The fresh air, the beautiful surroundings, and the varying terrain are a treat for rider and horse. To make sure it stays that way, there are some important rules to remember:

☼ As a beginner, never go on a trail ride alone. You should always be accompanied by an experienced rider or a guide.

☼ Always wear a helmet when you ride. Don't get careless and forget about it, particularly when you go on a trail ride. Wear clothing that will protect you from rain, wind, and scratchy branches.

☼ Check your tack. Bad equipment can't be replaced on the trail.

☼ Your pace should always be appropriate for the terrain. On blacktop and in snow and ice, you should only go at a walk so the horse doesn't slip. Also going downhill and the final stretch to the barn should be done at a walk.

☼ Be considerate of pedestrians, hikers, bicyclists, and automobile drivers.

.............12 READY FOR THE TEST

You have learned a whole lot since you started going to riding lessons, being around horses, taking care of them and riding them. That is very important. Horses are living beings that need to be handled properly. You probably already know that the inept handling of horses and unsafe riding can be dangerous to horse and rider.

Do you want to show what you know about horses and how well you can ride already? Then test yourself. Some countries offer horseback riding certificates and exams for young riders. Ask your riding instructor about that. Maybe there are some such tests you can take in your area.

But you and your friends can also come up with some tests of your own. Put together a quiz on horse facts, and add grooming and riding tasks. Your riding instructor or your parents will surely be happy to help you with it. Anyone who gets all of the correct answers of course receives a certificate and a medal. You can make these yourselves. Good luck!

On the following pages are some tips on what a beginning rider must know and must be able to do.

Basic horsemanship

These tasks are just about the horse.

There are two boxes after each line. Put an "x" in the first one if you think you already know something pretty well. Ask your riding instructor how he would rate you. Put an "x" in the second box if he gives you a good rating.
Now you can see exactly what you must still work on.

You must know this

- The specific behavior of horses, character.
- The safe handling of horses.
- Different horse breeds, sensory organs, anatomy.
- Options for the keeping of horses appropriate to the species.
- Good nutrition.
- Grooming and hoof care.
- Equipment.
- Equine health care, First Aid.
- Animal protection and responsibility for the horse.

You must be able to do this

- Talking to and safely approaching the horse.
- Leading and showing the horse, leading it past other horses.
- Securely tying the horse.
- Releasing the horse in the stall, paddock, or pasture.
- Grooming.
- Putting on wraps.
- Putting on saddle and bridle.
- Loading the horse in a trailer.

Riding

You must know this

- Most important facts about the seat.
- Riding aids.
- Dressage figures.

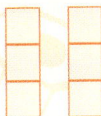

You must be able to do this

- Mounting and dismounting.
- Riding behind others and staying in line.
- Riding over cavaletti using side reins.
- Riding around obstacles using side reins.
- Riding in a dressage competition.
- Riding on the trail.
- Riding over cavaletti.
- Going over small jumps.

Of course you can't immediately do everything. Just continue setting bigger goals and you will gradually get better. Make sure the exercises match your skill level. Someone who has been practicing for a long time is of course better than a beginner.

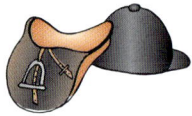

This is how you can get prepared

- Regularly go to your riding lessons and pay attention to what the instructor tells you.

- Take every opportunity to ask your riding instructor or other riders lots of questions.

- Read lots! There are many books about everything to do with horses, horse care, keeping and feeding horses.

- Take the opportunity to groom and tack up horses. Don't let others do your work, but help with it.

- Observe other riders as they interact with and ride their horses. You can learn from these role models. But you may notice mistakes and will want to do better yourself.

. . . . .13 THE FIRST HORSE SHOW

A horse show is an exiting event. The participants and their horses get well prepared far ahead of time. Then you can show what you have learned on the day of the show. You'll definitely enjoy competing against children your age or other children who have been practicing as much as you have. Surely your parents will pull for you and be happy about your achievements. The most successful horses receive ribbons and their riders get prizes, trophies, or small gifts. Surely you have dreamed of that.

But sometimes a show isn't as successful as planned. Don't get discouraged. Maybe you were too nervous, not well enough prepared, the horse was being difficult, or your competitors just were better this time. It's not that bad. Think about the possible reason and what you need to work on. Look forward to the next competition.

These are horse shows for beginning riders

Halter class

This test is primarily for little riders. The horse is led by a riding instructor, Mom, Dad, or an equestrian friend. The children demonstrate their seat at a walk and a trot.

Basic riding competition on the flat

This is a test for more advanced riders. Here, you show the horse, together with other riders, at a walk, trot, and canter. You are still permitted the use of side reins and the judges primarily grade your seat.

Basic show jumping competition

In this competition, you and your horse are required to complete a short jump course. There are usually six to eight jumps.

Record your first horse shows and your results here. You can also use a special notebook.

Date	Place	Name of Horse show	Results

Some competitions have a set course of events. But riding instructors can also make up some interesting competitions.

You'd probably really enjoy a course where you have to complete a variety of tasks. Together you can talk about it and make preparations.

Tasks for basic skills
- Lead the horse along a pre-drawn line on the ground.
- Turn the horse around in a marked space.
- Lead the horse past a bag of grain without stopping.
- Properly tie the horse and quickly untie it.
- Dismount in a specific spot and then remount.

Tasks for riding
- Ride a predetermined path in a particular gait.
- Ride around various silly obstacles.
- Jump your horse over various small obstacles.

Tasks for dexterity
- Write your name or your horse's name on a piece of paper while the horse is walking (or trotting).
- From horseback pick up a ball in a certain spot and throw it in a basket in another spot.

Scores are determined by points, number of mistakes, or time.

Write down your own ideas for small competitions here!

Preparing the horse

The horse is groomed thoroughly and its mane is braided and taped. Make sure you clean and condition the tack. Pack everything for the next day.

Preparing yourself

Lay out all the things you need for the next day. Riding helmet and boots are definitely mandatory. If you do not yet own an expensive uniform, wear a pair of light-colored pants and a dark form-fitting jacket. Make sure your clothes look neat. You should get plenty of sleep, get up on time and have a leisurely breakfast.

At the horse show

Allow plenty of time to tack up your horse before the test. This allows you to put everything on and gives you extra time in case something isn't working properly. Having to rush is not good for the horse or the rider. You'll need to warm up by walking and doing some calisthenics because cold muscles are stiff and don't work well. Your horse needs to warm up, too. You can warm him up in the schooling or cool-down area. You should also run through the most important exercises with your horse.

No matter how the show went, take care of your horse and reward it for its hard work!

......14 LITTLE HORSEBACK RIDING ENCYCLOPEDIA

Body Brush   The body brush is a soft brush used for grooming the horse. It should always be held in the hand pointing toward the horse's head.

Cavaletti   This is a low jump constructed from a pole with both ends nailed to a cross.

Center Line   This is the line that runs straight down the middle of the riding arena. It is where you go to mount up at the beginning of each riding lesson.

Chestnut   This is the fruit from a chestnut tree, but horses also have a chestnut. It is the rudimentary thumb, (horses walk on only one toe) which is located on the inside of each leg and consists of horn.

Colic   Colic is a severe stomachache in horses.

Course   Obstacles are set up in an indoor or outdoor arena for the horse and rider to jump over in a certain order. That order is referred to as a course.

Crop   This aid is held in the hand and is used to drive the horse forward. A whip is much longer than a crop and is used for lunging.

Cross Rail   This is a low jump constructed from two poles.

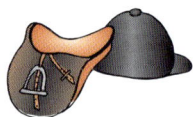

Eventing   In this discipline, you and your horse must be able to ride and have trained in dressage, jumping, and endurance.

Hand   Riding on the left hand doesn't mean that you should sit on your hand, but that you ride around the arena in the left direction (counter clockwise).

Jodhpurs   Jodhpurs are riding pants that are only worn with tall boots. Jodhpurs should be available at any equestrian store.

Martingale   A martingale is an aid rein that keeps the horse from throwing its head, but it doesn't restrict the neck to a particular position. It protects the horse from a rider's unsteady hand.

Side reins   Also called check reins, these are buckled to the saddle and clipped onto the snaffle ring as a rider's aid.

Pulling the reins out of your hands

The horse slowly stretches forward and downward until the reins are really long.

Putting on wraps

You wrap a part of your horse's leg with a bandage. You do this either because of an injury or for protection from external injuries while you ride.

Quadrille

Four, six, or eight riders perform a certain exercise at the same time. Maybe you have heard of the Spanish Riding School in Vienna, Austria. They always ride a quadrille in their performances.

Track

The track is the outermost line in the riding arena on which you usually ride during your lessons. There is also a second and third track, each approximately 4 to 6 feet closer to the center line.

Can you think of any additional terms that are important for the rider to know? Write them down here.

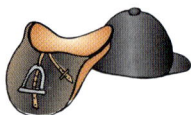

Hey, stop splashing!

. . . . .15 ANSWERS AND SOLUTIONS

Pg. 16   There are 15 horseshoes.

Pg. 20

1 ⟶ B
2 ⟶ C
3 ⟶ A

Pg. 28   Anything a horse lover and rider asks of his horse should be consistent with the horse's natural movements. Walking upright and ice skating are definitely not appropriate. Trying to teach the horse to do these things would be a stupid and ridiculous goal. You don't make your horse wear a skirt because you want it to look nice. That would only look silly.

Pg. 29   These are foods that in our opinion are not so healthy:
           Soda, fries, cake, hot dogs, candy
Of course, you can eat these foods, but you shouldn't eat them to often!

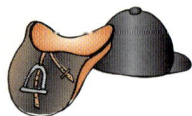

Pg. 39
1 Muzzle
2 Croup
3 Mane
4 Horseshoe
5 Nostrils
6 Tail
7 Withers

Pg. 42

1 The ears are turned back. The horse wants to hear what the little rider is saying.

2 The ears are alertly turned forward. There must be an interesting sound.

3 The horse is "flehming." Something smells strange.

4 The ears are flattened against the head and the head is extended forward. That looks aggressive!

5 The ears are turned forward. This horse also looks alert and is watching curiously.

Pg. 52
The pillow is of course nonsense! A riding helmet must be solid and shatter-proof

Pg. 58
1 The hair isn't tied back.
2 The jacket is too long.
3 The shoes are wrong.

Pg. 58
Horses 1 and 8 are identical.

Pg. 65
The horse will surely try to get those delicious apples. Can you assert yourself and lead your horse past?

Pg. 70

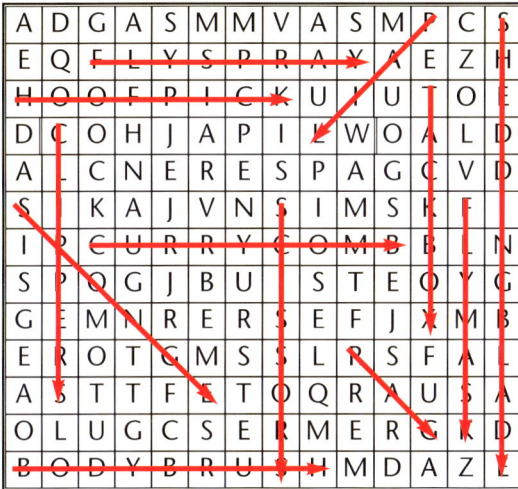

Pg. 71   The left horse it tied too short.
The right horse is tied too long. It could get tangled up in the long rope and injure itself.

Pg. 76   1   The rider isn't sitting up straight, but is leaning forward.
2   The rider is leaning too far back.
3   The rider sits lopsided in the saddle.
4   The rider's legs are up too high (chair seat).
5   The pelvis is tilted forward (split seat).

Pg. 78   1   The rider is sitting up too straight.
2   The elbows are too far back.
3   The reins are too long.
4   The reins are held too high.
5   The lower legs are too far back.

Pg. 85   The rider is bending at the hip, incorrectly shifting her weight.

Pg. 87
1 The hands are turned down.
2 The fists are rotated downward.
3 The hand is opened too far.
4 The hands are not level.
5 The reins are held too high.
6 The reins are too loose.

Pg. 99
Our ideas:
Cowboy, Indian, modern pentathlon athlete, carriage driver, polo player, mounted policeman, jockey, circus acrobat.

Pg. 104
There are several possibilities.
   One possibility is:

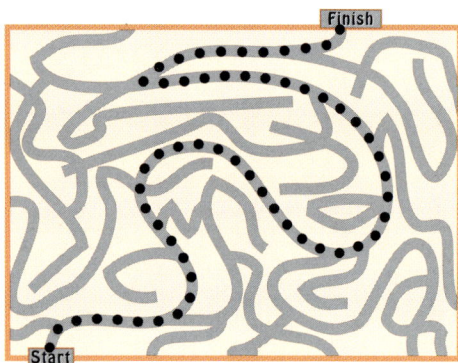

Pg. 110
Of course the marker can't be set up or drawn on the arena floor. It would be in the riders' way or get erased by all of the horses' feet stepping on it. The riders know that the X is in the exact center. They orientate themselves by the outer markings A, C, B and E.

16 Let's Talk

Dear horseback riding parents,

Do you remember when it began with your child; the longing glances at horses in the pasture and in the barn?

Your child has been bitten by the horse bug. It is great that you are willing to support him in learning this wonderful sport.

Horseback riding is very different from other sports or recreational activities. You need a horse to ride. The children learn right from the start to not just focus on their own person, but to also be solicitous and knowledgeable in caring for this creature. That's a lot of fun, means lots of responsibility, and is a big challenge. The positive character traits developed in horseback riding are also useful in school, as well as other areas of life.

In their riding lessons, the children learn from the start that our partner, the horse, is not just a cuddle animal, but that it needs assertiveness and firm leadership. That includes the handling of horses, as well as the correct seat and cuing.

Horseback riding allows children to feel their bodies in a whole new way. Becoming one with the movement of the horse, a sense of balance and harmony, coordination skills and a feel for rhythm and timing are all taught and practiced.

Children do not have the same attention span as adults. That is why children can not handle more than a 60-minute riding lesson. But there is a lot to do and see in the barn and the riding arena. Children can easily spend an entire afternoon there, meet friends, and they are in good hands.

Since the cost of horseback riding is quite high as compared to many other sports, you and your child should discuss this new hobby in depth. Why does he want to ride? Which riding stable would be best? Are the riding instructors well trained? Will my child feel comfortable there?

Help them, but do so cautiously! Don't expect more from your child than she is prepared to give at the moment. Don't compare him with other children of the same age, but praise your child's individual progress. Also, remember that much depends on the quality of the lesson horse.

Maybe you will soon have a little bookworm at home who wants to get lots of information on her favorite hobby. In addition to using our book as a support tool for learning to ride, we would like it to inspire a varied interest in horses and riding.

Ok, I've done enough of these preliminary exercises. I'm ready for a real horse now!

LET'S TALK

Dear riding instructor,

Surely you'll agree that it is a great feeling to see these little guys standing in front of you with their faces full of suspense and their eyes full of expectation. Now it is up to you to introduce them to horses and horseback riding.

But each child is different. There are the self-confident ones and the scared ones, the diligent ones and those less diligent, the talented and the less talented. Each child is a unique individual with individual qualifications and a unique developmental background, with hopes and desires, with existential orientations and needs. All of them deserve our attentiveness.

Children want to be active, move around and have fun. A group setting in particular allows them to compete with others their own age and spur each other on. For beginning riders, the most important role model is their riding instructor. They watch everything carefully: how he handles the horses, how he talks to them, and also how he might, for instance, adhere to the safety rules.

The young rider herself is what's most important in the teaching and learning process. The child, no matter how young and even as a total beginner, is always subject to its own development and never just an object of our influence. Promote and put to use the independence of your little beginning riders. Take the path from instructing to inspiring. Children can and should, rather than must and have to.

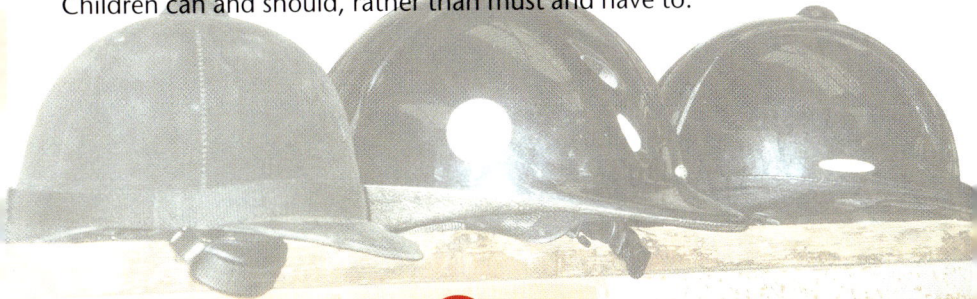

What a riding instructor must have for children:

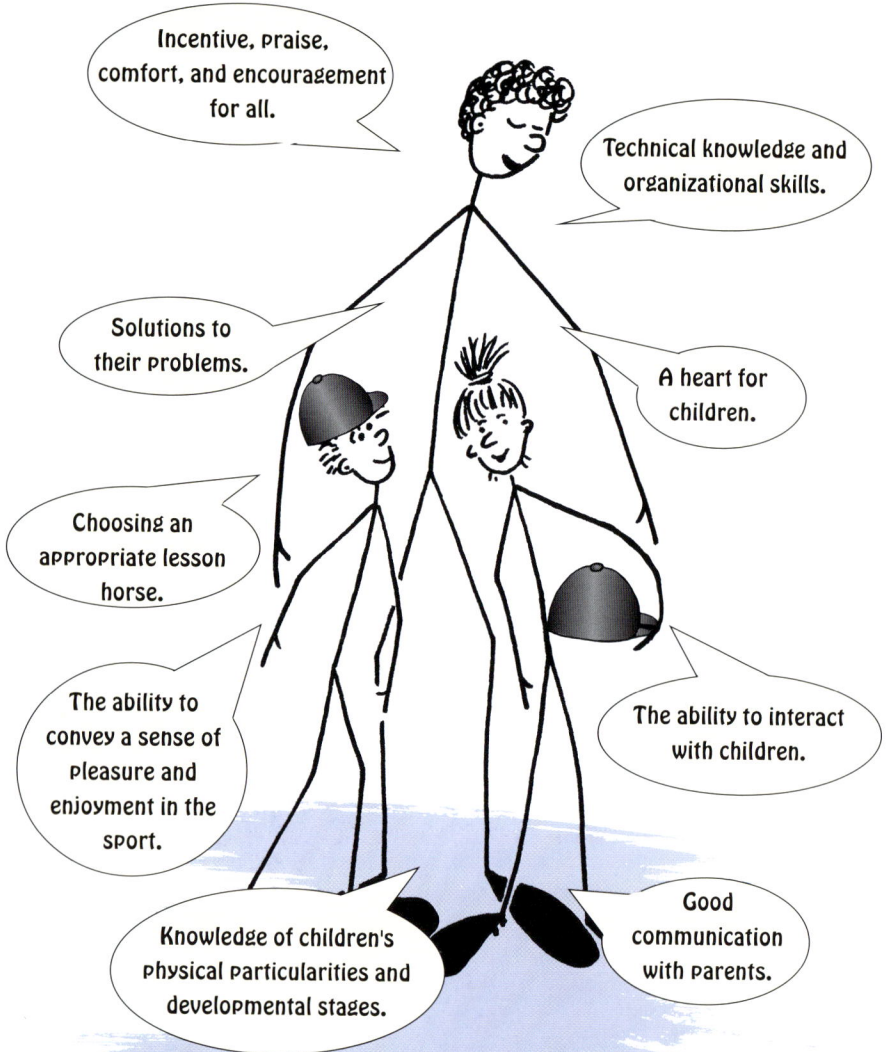

Incentive, praise, comfort, and encouragement for all.

Technical knowledge and organizational skills.

Solutions to their problems.

A heart for children.

Choosing an appropriate lesson horse.

The ability to convey a sense of pleasure and enjoyment in the sport.

The ability to interact with children.

Knowledge of children's physical particularities and developmental stages.

Good communication with parents.

The value of this little book

The value of this book depends entirely on how you incorporate it into the horseback riding training. It is written specifically for children who are beginning horseback riding. But it is also recommended for parents who want to accompany their child on this path.

This book focuses on the children's needs and is intended to help them get involved with horses and riding outside of the riding arena and barn, as well. The illustrations and descriptions in the book provide the child with a sizable basis of information for practicing.

He or she will be able to follow your instructions and demonstrations more easily. The young riders can review at their leisure things they have learned, record goals and advances in learning, while getting suggestions for practicing at home and with other children. This helps promote independent action and speeds up the learning process.

An environment is created in which the children are encouraged to think step by step about their practicing and learning, their movements and actions, and finally to examine and evaluate their performance. They become the riding instructor's partner. We want children to enjoy coming to their riding lessons and go home with a sense of success. And that of course makes the practice sessions more fun for the riding instructor, as well.

The book at riding lessons

☺ Tell the children that this book is their personal companion in learning horseback riding. Give them the club logo and take a photo to paste in the book. This promotes bonding with you and the club.

☺ Help the children to use the book properly. Start out by reading sections together and explain to them how to view and understand the pictures and illustrations. Together with your students make entries on goals, suggestions, etc. By doing so, you provide the children with important orientation guides for understanding and independent practice.

☺ You can also use the book to give a little homework for the next riding lesson. The children read about a topic and then get to demonstrate and talk about it at the next lesson.

We wish you and your little protégées lots of fun, enjoyment, and of course lots of horseback riding successes.

. . . .Photo and Illustration Credits

Cover Design: Jens Vogelsang

Illustrations: Katrin Barth

Cover Photo: U 1 – Sportpressephoto Bongarts, Hamburg
U 4 – Katrin Barth

Photos (inside):   Gabo, Eva Lempa-Röller, Manfred Sendelbeck, Renate Sieber

HORSEBACK

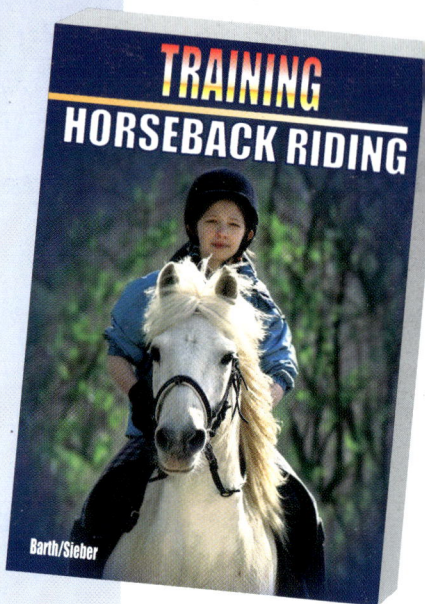

Katrin Barth / Antonia Sieber

Training Horseback Riding

is written for children and adolescents who have learned to ride and are beginning to train. It is intended as a training companion and work book.

The question: "Training – but how?" is answered in an age appropriate and sophisticated manner.

As in the book "Learning Horseback Riding", the little horse "Max" accompanies the reader throughout the book, and offers tips and suggestions, even for exercises outside of the riding arena.

c. 152 pages, full color print
15 photos, 30 illustrations
Paperback, $5^3/_4$ " x $8^1/_4$ "
c. £ 9,95 UK / $ 14,95 US
$ 20,95 CDN / € 14,95

ISBN: 1-84126-156-4

MEYER
MEYER
SPORT